The Education Adviser

Raising the quality of education advice and support

The Role of the Education Adviser

ASSOCIATION of EDUCATION ADVISERS

CRITICAL PUBLISHING

THE EDUCATION ADVISER SERIES

Take a look at all the titles in this series.

- *The Role of the Education Adviser*
- *Advising on School Improvement*
- *Advising on Governance in Education*
- *Advising on Organisational Development in Education*
- *Advising on Change Management in Education*
- *Advising on Implementing Quality Systems in Education*

Acknowledgements

The development of the AoEA book series and this first volume, in particular, is an important milestone for the Association. The range of chapters capture the innovative work of our Associates and friends of our organisation but they crystallise the journey of the AoEA which has included the construction of criteria, establishing processes of accreditation and widespread professional learning and conversation. This book from a wide range of perspectives captures the energy, debates and approaches at the heart of advisory work.

With this in mind I'd like to extend my thanks to the editorial team, to each of our authors and to the publishing team who, in a very short period of time have contributed to bringing this book to publication. A huge amount of energy, reflection and craft has gone into creating such an engaging and varied text which is hugely appreciated.

Les Walton, CBE
Executive Chair of the AoEA

First published in 2024 by Critical Publishing Ltd

British Library Cataloguing in Publication Data
A CIP record for this book is available from the British Library

ISBN: 978-1-915713-93-3

This book is also available in the following e-book formats:
EPUB ISBN: 978-1-915713-94-0
Adobe e-book ISBN: 978-1-915713-95-7

Text and cover design by Out of House Limited
Project Management by Newgen Publishing UK

Critical Publishing
3 Connaught Road
St Albans
AL3 5RX

www.criticalpublishing.com

Contents

About the AoEA and the editorial team

About the AoEA

Our vision is that every school, college and education provider has access to high-quality support, advice and challenge, which is independent and focused on improving outcomes for children, schools and their communities.

Our mission is to provide an accredited quality standard, to offer continuous professional learning and to create a community for those who support and challenge schools, colleges and other education providers.

About the editorial team

Dr Tony Birch, Series Editor

Tony is author of Primary Education as a Whole *and Founding Director of Birch Education, an educational consultancy dedicated to empowering individuals and teams to develop high quality, sustainable approaches. Previously Tony worked for Bolton Council for more than 20 years: as a school improvement adviser and head of school improvement before becoming the lead for education and learning strategy.*

Ian Lane, Chair of the Editorial Team

Following headship of an inner-city secondary school, Ian joined a local authority advisory service as a Senior Adviser and was later appointed Director of School Improvement for the same 'core city'. In more recent years, he has held CEO roles in both a primary and a secondary schools' multi-academy trust and worked as an independent school improvement adviser.

Les Walton, CBE, Executive Chair of the AoEA

Les' career spans pivotal changes in education since the 1960s. His book, Education: The Rock and Roll Years *is described by Professor Andy Hargreaves as 'visionary ... An excellent piece of writing'. Les has been a Headteacher, Director of Education and Founder and Principal of a Further Education college. He has also had significant regional and national influence. He founded Northern Education Associates and Schools North-East. Nationally, he chaired the Young People's Learning Agency and assisted its transition to the Education and Skills Funding Agency. He has also been a key adviser to multiple UK Secretaries of State. Les received the OBE in 1996 and CBE in 2013 for his services to education.*

Eric Halton, Non-Executive Director of the AoEA

Over a period of 13 years, Eric's leadership in primary headships significantly improved inclusive provision, high-quality outcomes for children, resulting in outstanding inspection ratings. During this time, he also held a number of school-to-school system roles as consultant to individual schools, building professional practice networks. Eric, in more recent years, was head of a highly regarded school inspection and advisory service, which spanned more than one local authority.

Mary Lowery, Head of School Improvement, Northern Ireland

Mary has over 20 years' teaching experience in two urban integrated comprehensive colleges in Derry and Belfast and has been part of the development of integrated education in Northern Ireland since its early days. Mary joined the Education and Training Inspectorate (ETI) in 2014, inspecting across educational phases and supporting the development of models of inspection and self-evaluation, before moving into school development work with the Education Authority in 2018. In 2019, she co-founded WomenEdNI, which connects and inspires women in educational leadership.

Mairéad Mhig Uaid, Head of School and System Improvement, Northern Ireland

Mairéad has 20 years' experience in school senior leadership, bringing about both school and system-wide improvement. Her experience extends beyond organisational settings to design and delivery of tailored curriculum, resource and Teacher Professional Learning. Mairéad leads school and system improvement through a people-centric coaching style.

Peter Parish, AoEA Development Team

Peter formerly led a School Improvement Service in a local authority in the North-East of England. During this time the Council was awarded Beacon Council status for 'Tackling School Failure'. He also co-ordinated successful funding proposals for major education projects. He then became Head of Planning, Commissioning and Quality Assurance in the council's Children's Services. In 2010 he became Director of Operations for a large multi-academy trust.

Lauren Hanson, AoEA Central Team Support

Lauren is currently completing a graduate internship programme set up by Sunderland University, and has been with the AoEA since September 2022. Lauren runs the AoEA Professional Learning Programme for education advisers, which provides both online and face to face seminars as well as fortnightly Education Keeping In Touch (EduKIT) meetings throughout the academic year. She works alongside members of the AoEA Development Team, as well as several external experts, to ensure that the programme runs smoothly.

About the contributors

Dame Kathy August, Non-Executive Director of the AoEA

Kathy has spent 45 years working in and for public education. She has been a Director of Education in two LEAs, worked as a senior adviser in the DfE, been a visiting professor at Salford Business School, and worked as an interim CEO. She became a Dame in 2014 for her services to education.

Debi Bailey, CEO for the Newcastle East Multi-Academy Trust

Debi Bailey is CEO of the NEAT multi-academy trust, which comprises both primary and secondary schools. Debi is a National Leader of Education and has over 28 years of primary school experience. She believes passionately in working with families, carers and wider stakeholders in providing, in partnership with her schools' communities, the best possible education and life chances for their young people.

Frazer Bailie, School Improvement Professional, Education Authority, Northern Ireland

Frazer has worked as a School Improvement Professional in the Education Authority Northern Ireland since 2019. He has a strong track record of working with disadvantaged communities and earned a Pearson Primary Principal of the Year Award in 2010. He has also served as an associate inspector, a leadership lecturer and a chief moderator for the Curriculum Council.

Martyn Beales, School Improvement Manager, Hampshire City Council

Martyn is a School Improvement Manager for Hampshire County Council, overseeing an advisory team as well as contributing to county strategy. He has advised schools and MATs across England and worked for Oxfordshire County Council. Martyn has held leadership roles in primary schools and was previously a Primary Phase Inspector/Adviser.

Karen Bramwell, CEO of Forward as One Multi-Academy Trust

Karen is founding CEO of Forward As One multi-academy trust. She became a National Leader of Education in 2011 and was Leadership Director for the Greater Manchester Challenge. Karen regularly provides training to headteachers across the country and is an NPQEL facilitator (National Professional Qualification for Executive Leaders). In 2019, Karen was awarded the Women in Leadership Award by 'She inspires'.

Mike Buchanan, Founder of PositivelyLeading

Mike is the founder of PositivelyLeading, a strategic support consultancy for school and college leaders and school groups. He was recently Executive Director of HMC, the world's oldest headteacher association. At Ashford School, he oversaw its transformation from a small girls' school to a thriving, all-age, co-educational day/boarding school for over a thousand pupils.

Dr Louis DeLoreto, Principal of EO Smith High School, USA

Dr Louis DeLoreto is in his 22nd year as the principal of EO Smith High School in Storrs, Connecticut. His PhD research has led to an increased understanding of the importance of the awareness of the lasting impact of school suspension and alternative strategies to reduce suspensions, particularly for students at-risk. In 2022, E.O. Smith High School earned national recognition and received the 2022 National Blue Ribbon Award for overall improvements in student performance across 13 areas, including for students identified as 'high needs of intervention'.

Tom Grieveson, AoEA Development Team

Tom has extensive experience of school and system-wide improvement and inspection. He worked as a senior HMI (Her Majesty's Inspector) with Ofsted within the North-East Yorkshire and Humberside senior leadership team. He has consistently led some of the most high-profile section 5 and section 8 inspections in several parts of England. Prior to joining HMI, Tom was a headteacher in two schools covering a 12-year period and held senior positions in local authority school improvement teams, including as Head of Service.

Professor Andy Hargreaves, Research Professor, Boston College, USA

Professor Andy Hargreaves is Visiting Professor at the University of Ottawa and Research Professor at Boston College. He has been honoured in Canada, the US, and UK for services to public education. He is a member of the US National Academy of Education and advises the First Minister of Scotland. Andy has written many books, his most recent of which are Leadership from the Middle; *and* The Age of Identity *(with Dennis Shirley).*

Alix Jackson, Vice Principal of Hazelwood Integrated College, Northern Ireland

Alix is Vice Principal at Hazelwood Integrated College, having fulfilled a number of leadership roles throughout her time in education, covering the full range of pastoral and academic responsibilities. Alix also served as Transformation Coordinator for Glengormley High School from December 2019, prior to taking up post as Vice Principal at Hazelwood Integrated College in March 2021.

Eithne Leming, School Improvement Consultant

Eithne has worked as an Education Adviser and consultant since 2007. Her work includes school improvement work for the National Strategies, academy trusts and for a range of maintained primary and special schools. She has held LA roles for SEND, Looked After Children and for primary assessment as KS1/2 moderation manager. She is a highly skilled school improvement adviser and coach.

Kevin McDermid, AoEA Development Team

Kevin has over 25 years of senior leadership experience in secondary schools, including two headships of inner-city comprehensive schools, and a sixth form college. He has a secondary school background and was Teaching Awards Head Teacher of the Year for the North-East & Cumbria in 2004–5. Kevin has extensive experience as a school improvement specialist, adviser and independent consultant. He has worked with many individual schools, and numerous LAs and multi-academy trusts across the North of England. Latterly, he was appointed as CEO of a MAT in the North-East.

Professor Dame Alison Peacock, CEO of the Chartered College of Teaching

Professor Dame Alison Peacock is Chief Executive of the Chartered College of Teaching, a Professional Body that seeks to empower a knowledgeable and respected teaching profession through membership and accreditation. Prior to joining the Chartered College, Alison was Executive Headteacher of The Wroxham School in Hertfordshire.

Introduction to the AoEA and the purpose of the book series

LES WALTON, CBE

The purpose of the book is to support the professional learning of those who are involved in education and providing support to others, including (i) those currently engaged as leaders in educational settings; and (ii) those who are advising and supporting them.

As we move deeper into the third decade of the twenty-first century, the need to redesign the process by which schools are supported and enabled to improve has become increasingly important. In 2016, a meeting was held in the Department for Education headquarters in London. Key national school and college representative organisations were present. All agreed that there was a need to quality assure and develop the quality of advice and support that schools receive.

Following an intensive research and development programme it was decided to establish the Association of Education Advisers (AoEA), which is independent of national and local government. It was also decided that the AoEA should provide an accredited international standard which would be relevant to all schools, colleges and education providers across the UK and, ultimately, throughout the world.

The AoEA has a vision that every school and college, no matter their size or designation, has access to high-quality support, advice and challenge which is independent and focused on improving outcomes for children and young people, their schools, their colleges and their communities.

There are 36,000 schools across the UK alone. The core message from those who support and advise on school improvement to those who lead and inspect is that we should 'professionalise' the role of the adviser. A major part of the work of the AoEA has been in developing the professional community within the UK and internationally for those who support and advise schools, colleges and other education providers.

This accredited national and international community of advisers is increasing by the day. We believe that we are at the very beginning of our journey and that at the outset we seriously underestimated the potential of an international community of education advisers. We don't any more!

We believe that those who lead, inspect and advise schools should have access to accredited standards and continuous professional learning. The three points of this triangular relationship are all necessary. If one part is weakened, then the whole system becomes unsustainable.

Advising and supporting colleagues within schools and colleges over which you may not have direct power and control requires a unique set of skills and knowledge. The hundreds of educationalists who have achieved the AoEA accredited standard tell us that they value most highly the independent nature of the AoEA, the opportunity to reflect on their work through a rigorous accreditation process and associated professional learning. They tell us that the AoEA process provides:

- an opportunity to reflect on their own practice through external eyes and to condense and showcase their contribution to organisational improvement;

- a valuable opportunity to receive external affirmation and feedback while also having signposted opportunities for further learning.

It helps them to:

- validate their ability to advise others;

- understand their own skills and expertise in relation to how they can support others;

- develop further and hone their skills and expertise in supporting others;

- make others aware of their knowledge, skills and experience, thereby strengthening the educational advisory network and potential for increased learning and support from one another.

In harnessing the strengths of our growing membership, this series of books entitled 'The Education Adviser' will provide some of the most up-to-date thinking and examples of good practice from across the

UK and internationally. If you provide advice and support or lead a school and college, then the aim of this series of books is to provide some essential reading. The AoEA has selected contributors from the 400-plus accredited AoEA Associates and partners, together with well-known experts from across the UK and beyond.

All contributors have mastery in their specific area, whether it is in how to demonstrate professional credibility, understanding what causes a school's success or failure, developing a school improvement strategy, supporting major change programmes or using quality improvement tools such as Kaizen.

The books in this series are:

1. *The Role of the Education Adviser*

2. *Advising on School Improvement*

3. *Advising on Governance in Education*

4. *Advising on Organisational Development in Education*

5. *Advising on Change Management in Education*

6. *Advising on Implementing Quality Systems in Education*

This book, *The Role of the Education Adviser*, is the first in our series. We hope you will enjoy reading it and that it contributes to your professional learning and role as an education adviser, wherever you may be working, in supporting and advising school and college leaders.

Introduction to Book 1: *The Role of the Education Adviser* – a repertoire of skills and approaches

DR TONY BIRCH

The eclectic selection of chapters in this book illustrates the powerful influence of the education adviser: it is rich with examples of the variety, vitality, impact and innovation emerging from advisory work. The AoEA's six criteria relating to skills and knowledge underpin this. Successfully advising for impact requires advisers with:

- strong personal attributes and skills;

- an ability to offer considered challenge;

- the ability to enable others through support and expertise;

- the capacity to enable transference of knowledge;

- the ability to do this through the credibility and earned authority developed in their field.

Throughout the chapters we see education advisers as vital enablers working within and across a complex system.

The role of the education adviser often flies beneath the radar when thinking about school improvement: the emphasis is often, rightly, towards debates around leadership, curriculum and pedagogy, inclusion and achievement, for example. Yet the adviser's contribution to the education system is highly significant and found in many forms both within and across schools. Very often the influence and impact of the adviser is difficult to quantify because they operate in so many different ways (through coaching and mentoring, challenging performance and evaluation, for example), across multitudinous contexts and layers (from the classroom all the way to ministerial level). The adviser's work is so closely interwoven with the organisations they support and because it is the success of those organisations that counts, they are much less visible. This book brings the adviser to the surface through contributions that are both analytical and illustrative. The chapters explore the role of the education adviser, detailing the attributes and approaches they need in order to be successful. The book also highlights their impact in the field, where authors describe their journeys through complex educational challenges and the way they have brought about change.

Book structure and content

Les Walton's introductory chapter illustrates how 'advice' has been woven into the education system in different forms over a number of years and how advice and guidance forms a key component that supports decision making and development across education systems. He argues that '*if we are to develop a self-managing school system, then the advice schools are offered must be of the highest quality, rigorously validated, independent and primarily designed to serve the needs of our children and our schools*'. He is signalling a vital role, aiming '*to provide support and guidance to schools and colleges in their efforts to improve overall performance and enhance the quality of education*'. The remainder of the book builds upon this.

Part 1 of this book explores the importance of the role of the education adviser and the chapters are a mix of think pieces underpinning how we provide advisory support and practice. It considers the qualities and features of highly effective advice, exemplifying why it is important, skilfully delivered and powerful in affecting change. Part 2 contextualises this through illustrative examples of advisers leading and supporting change.

Part 1: the role of the education adviser

Tom Grieveson's contribution opens the first part of the book, exploring the similarities and differences between advising and inspection. He identifies two key pillars that underpin an adviser's effectiveness: their understanding of causation in an institution's performance and the capacity to make improvements happen and to sustain this over time. They are, he argues, underpinned by the adviser's authoritative influence, which emerges from their professional credibility.

Kevin McDermid's subsequent chapter describes this through his own personal experiences as he illustrates the practice of advisory work, using this to explain why the AoEA was formed. He clearly describes the repertoire of the education adviser and their contribution to the '*ongoing longitudinal journey of improvement within educational settings*' achieved through, for example, mentoring, performance management, coaching, training, ongoing advice, constructive criticism, motivating and persuading – a not inconsiderable repertoire.

Eithne Leming's account exemplifies Kevin's contribution. She drills into the personal attributes and the sophisticated communication skills she needed while undertaking a sensitive investigation, describing how she established '*a level of trust and confidence in the process and in my own ability to remain a fair and independent investigator*'.

The skills of the adviser are also illustrated in Martyn Beales' chapter, where effective communication is explored as he explains how a complex 'advisory' report must be skilfully crafted and have a transparent character if it is to both 'land' effectively and, in his terms, '*add value*'. These chapters collectively start to reveal the approaches, skills and qualities associated with effective advisory work.

The chapters which follow acknowledge that advisers must add value through their work and bring about change: each recognises that there will be barriers along the way. Les Walton's second contribution builds upon this by exploring the idea of challenge. The effective education adviser must be able to provide challenge coupled closely with insight and sensitivity if they are to affect change. Challenge is part of a repertoire of approaches; he develops an argument for what he terms '*supportive intervention*'.

Dr Louis DeLoreto meanwhile recognises directly that advisers will meet with resistance along the way. His positive approach recommends finding and embracing the resistance, keeping the focus on what we can control and instilling a sense of urgency for continuous change. He points us to important advisory qualities that include curiosity, confidence, courage and resolve.

These chapters lead well into Eric Halton's chapter, which acts as a reminder that working closely with a school's leadership team leads to maximum impact – what he calls working in 'concert'. Impact, therefore, emerges '*from co-construction with school leaders*'. Eric's contribution celebrates authenticity; in his words: '*Put simply, leaders respond best when they can feel that external advisers will challenge but are also professionally invested in the school's success*' and '*working collectively with leaders to bring about improvement matters to them*'.

The chapters so far in this section have focused on advisory skills and knowledge. The next three chapters explain how a focus on advisory skills and knowledge can have systemic benefits. Professor Dame Alison Peacock's account is written from her position as Chief Executive of the Chartered College of Teaching. In the context of the English education system, she argues '*for a profession inspired by the importance of phronesis, professional intuitive wisdom informed by relevant and important research, supported and enabled by a compassionate tier of educational advisers*'.

Illustratively, Mary Lowery's account explores how she led a strategic approach to advice within the education system of Northern Ireland. She demonstrates how the Education Authority is proactively '*growing a system-wide high-quality advisory community, engaging colleagues, educational partners and school leaders*'. She describes its impact: '*opening conversations, building relationships, collegiality and trust across the system, raising the level of professional dialogue and bringing a degree of coherence to how we approach school development*'.

Lastly, Professor Andy Hargreaves describes his experiences as an international adviser, reminding us that 'advice' is to be found globally and a phenomenon not just within but across education systems. His is also a reminder of moral purpose: as he puts it, '*It should be about the millions of young people whose lives you have a glorious opportunity to help improve.*'

Collectively, these chapters offer a reminder that a strong system of 'advice' in an education system can become an important lever for change and improvement.

Part 2: the adviser in action

The second part of the book showcases some of the myriad examples that characterise the power of education advisers, together with their impact on children and young people and their communities: each is firmly located in the 'action'. The varied contexts and challenges open out to reveal creative and sustainable approaches that are carefully attuned to context.

The first four chapters focus on inclusion and partnership development, while the latter two demonstrate the different yet complementary approaches that highly experienced and professionally credible advisers took as they approached school improvement challenges, all six demonstrating impact and sustainability.

Advisory skills and knowledge 'sing' when creating powerful partnerships. Frazer Bailie describes addressing disadvantage in a powerful account of how he worked with his local community in Northern Ireland:

> *The ambition was to create a partnership to work "upstream". The aim was to address the causes of underachievement and not just the symptoms. Put simply, the desire was for these children and young people to thrive.*

He recognises the success of this work and the harnessing of commitment: '*Its origins come from a purposeful conversation among a group of invested participants who wanted things to change*'. Alix Jackson's account of transformation to an 'integrated' school is no less inspiring. Also set in Northern Ireland, she reveals how persuading, guiding and influencing are powerful processes that depend heavily on trust. Continuing in this vein, Debi Bailey, Chief Executive of NEAT Multi-Academy Trust in England, reveals how she acted as an 'enabler' and built expertise through 'knowledge transfer' to address an identified need which she describes as

> *to support families, make effective use of the resources available and work to ensure the best possible outcomes for our young people.*

Powerfully, she describes the successful outcome as a '*holistic, compassionate and successful approach to working with our families*'.

The second set of chapters focuses on approaches to school improvement. Karen Bramwell is Chief Executive of Forward As One Multi-Academy Trust, and her account explores how she has grown a community of 'generous' leaders. She describes the process by which her advice has

> *created a series of "communities" of effective leaders, underpinned by the strength of a shared social contract, supported by generous, effective school leaders who have deep relationships with, and responsibility for, one another.*

In particular, her own professional credibility can be seen as a vital vehicle for this community.

This rich repertoire of approaches, recognising that there are differences in approach, all reveal a deep understanding of the qualities which lead to impact and lasting, sustainable success. Mike Buchanan discusses an approach to school improvement which applied to a specific set of circumstances, describing it as the '*hard, slow and satisfying way*'. This very personal account describes Mike's beliefs about change, leading him to conclude that:

> *The purpose of advising is to improve both personal and organisational performance so that our children and young people achieve to their optimum. Great advising is demanding of both the adviser and those engaging with the advice. Change only becomes transformation when it is sustained and demonstrated by the behaviours of people, which takes time to become truly embedded.*
>
> *Transformation is slow, hard but ever so satisfying!*

Finally, Dame Kathy August brings the book to a conclusion as she describes her self-awareness as an adviser, recognising the differences between leadership and advice when supporting governance in recruiting a new leader. She describes how she successfully enabled improvement in three phases: by analysing and explaining; absorbing and appreciating; and, finishing, tapering and fading her involvement.

Collectively, this book reveals advising in all of its rich tapestry, drawing on advisers from a range of backgrounds. The final chapter, written by Dr Tony Birch and Ian Lane, summarises the key messages of this book for those involved in advisory work. I hope you enjoy reading this book as much as we have enjoyed writing it with a number of highly regarded specialists in their field.

Part 1: the role of the education adviser

1 The role of the education adviser: an English and a historical perspective

LES WALTON, CBE

As a key principle, we have sought to learn from the past and understand how the role of the education adviser has changed over time. This has helped to inform our understanding of what it means to be an education adviser. This role, we believe, will also continue to evolve as the membership grows and as we embrace an increasingly diverse and international community of education advisers.

In learning from the past in England, and we understand that it may well be different elsewhere, ever since local authorities were established schools have been receiving visits from officers of the local authority. Some would be there to provide a link with the local authority, others to inspect the school on behalf of the local authority and the remainder to provide advice for subjects, for specific themes or for the school or the college as an organisation.

The best education advisers have always played an important and honourable role within the education sector. Over the years, they have been deployed under a range of different role descriptions: as School Improvement Partners, National Challenge Advisers or National Leaders in Education, to name but three. Nowadays, there are numerous specialist advisers, covering different types of schools and offering different specialisms, including governance, change management, finance and people development.

An education adviser can work in numerous ways with schools but, primarily, they are there to support the school's ability to plan for, review and implement educational strategy.

During the 1970s and 1980s, local authorities in England employed a significant number of advisers, particularly subject advisers. They were mainly former heads of department who had decided to pursue a different career path from the within-school traditional route of deputy headship (followed often by headship) by choosing to work for the local authority more directly.

Headteachers were also routinely allocated a 'school adviser', who was specifically linked with the school and primarily worked directly with them and possibly other link schools.

Many subject teachers, heads of subject departments, in particular, placed considerable value on the opportunity to talk to the local authority subject adviser, primarily using them as a sounding board for ideas and developments. The interaction was very straightforward: the subject advisers would bring with them the latest thinking and information about subject-specific requirements. In addition, they would also run training programmes, primarily focusing on the knowledge and skills that subject departments required.

This system worked reasonably well until the early 1990s, when local management of schools began and the Office for Standards in Education, Children's Services and Skills (Ofsted) was introduced. The relationship with advisers, who were often asked to take on a more inspectorial role, began to change significantly and headteachers began to suggest that local authority advisers who had no experience of running a school might not, in the new era, be able to properly support and challenge them.

When I became a director of education, the local authority began increasingly to involve headteachers to work as advisers. I subsequently introduced this model to Bradford, where we called these headteachers 'School Improvement Partners'. In Bradford we began by selecting a team of outstanding headteachers to work with schools in very challenging contexts.

The Department for Education (DfE) then considered spreading this advisory model across the whole of the UK and asked Newcastle local authority and Northern Education (which I founded) to lead one of the national pilots. The model that we put forward in our pilot required the advisers to be 'relatively independent' of the local authority and the school, and thereby to be in a position to challenge and support both the school and the local authority in the best interests of the children and young people. I remember attending a meeting at the DfE where headteacher representatives vigorously argued for the independence of School Improvement Partners from local authorities, while the representative of local authorities, equally enthusiastically, suggested that they should report directly to the local authority. In the end, the government decided that School Improvement Partners would be funded by the DfE and commissioned by local authorities. However, some local authorities supported the Newcastle model of relative autonomy for School Improvement Partners.

Despite DfE guidelines in 2004 stating that the School Improvement Partners were required to respect the autonomy of the school, most School Improvement Partners nationally were seen as officers of the local authority.

As an additional development, in 2006, the National College for School Leadership began to identify serving headteachers who had achieved excellent results in their schools. They were to be called National Leaders in Education. This was clearly a significant step towards maintaining advisory independence from the local authorities. Of course, this model was funded by national government and could never be seen as truly independent.

Later, in 2008, the then Secretary of State launched the £400m National Challenge programme, which was to target the 638 lowest-performing schools nationally. At the same time, 70 of these schools would become academies by September 2010. The central government control over school advisers was clearly being strengthened. National Challenge Advisers, a key component of the National Challenge programme, were then appointed to work with the targeted schools.

The direction changed radically in 2010, when the new coalition government announced that the statutory requirement for local authorities to commission School Improvement Partners was to be removed and the funding withdrawn. At the same time, the DfE closed down the National Challenge programme and widened the academisation programme to include high-performing schools.

Schools to date continue to receive advice from the Office of the Regional Director, the local authority or relevant providing body, or from advisers they commission themselves. Yet these advisers do not have to conform to any national standard for education advisers working with schools. There is no national quality assurance or accreditation of advisers beyond the work of Ofsted, which is essentially inspectorial.

In 2016, in discussing the issue of school advisers with the then Under-Secretary of State for Education, I suggested that there was a significant gap in the system. There already exists a qualification for school leaders and a quality standard for Ofsted inspectors. Additionally, schools are obliged to use accredited accountants regarding their financial affairs. Yet there exists this significant gap in the lack of any accreditation for those who are tasked with advising schools.

In 2017, the Association of Education Advisers (AoEA) was launched. The concept received a great deal of support nationally. This development was inspired by the simple belief that those who advise, either on behalf of national and local government, trusts, federations or individual schools, should be accredited, developed and trained with the same rigour as our school leaders and inspectors. In effect, the new body established national quality standards, which are independent of government and designed for educational specialists who can both support and challenge schools.

If we are to develop a self-managing school system, then the advice schools are offered must be of the highest quality, rigorously validated, independent and primarily designed to serve the needs of our children and our schools.

The role of the education adviser is to provide support and guidance to schools and colleges in their efforts to improve overall performance and enhance the quality of education. The role of the education adviser can range from a school leader who provides support to a colleague within another school to a full-time professional undertaking this function with one or across many schools. The adviser typically works with school leaders, teachers and staff to identify areas for improvement, develop action plans and implement strategies that will lead to positive change.

Identifying and developing the unique and distinctive role of the education adviser has been at the heart of our development and much of our thinking has evolved over the last few years. We have considered all aspects of the role of the adviser: from the initial development of the accreditation criteria, bringing a new focus on governance and quality systems, to an analysis of the difference between the transactional role of the adviser and the statutory, distinctive roles of the inspector and school leader.

We have developed new thinking in relation to the role of the education adviser, which we have sought to bring together via an accreditation process and a professional learning offer addressing key areas of an education adviser's work. In this book and the series of books which will follow, you will be introduced to how education advisers can hone their professional credibility, improve their efficacy, address the complex world of governance, develop organisations, support the management of change and assist in building quality improvement within and across schools and colleges.

Key criteria

In this first book, *The Role of the Education Adviser*, the content is underpinned by the following key criteria:

1. demonstrating personal attributes and skills;
2. ability to challenge and work within agreed protocols;
3. acting as an enabler by providing support to drive delivery;
4. enabling knowledge transfer through reference to up-to-date exemplars;
5. demonstrating authority and professional credibility with clients.

These criteria are brought to life by specialists with mastery in their field. The chapters include exemplification of how the authors' skills as education advisers have brought about improved provision in their work with school leaders.

2 Distinguishing between the role of the adviser and the inspector: exposing the debate

TOM GRIEVESON

Key learning

- While both inspectors and advisers are focused on improving the life chances of children and young people, this chapter seeks to prompt discussion about their respective roles and how these are carried out.

- This chapter aims to distil the distinctive elements of each role while acknowledging where there is commonality, most evident in the skill sets required to undertake both kinds of work.

AoEA criteria

- Criterion 2. Ability to challenge and work within agreed protocols.

- Criterion 3. Acting as an enabler by providing support to drive delivery.

- Criterion 5. Demonstrating authority and professional credibility with clients.

Introduction

This chapter is designed to promote discussion about the respective roles undertaken by school advisers and school inspectors. While it attempts to bring a degree of clarity in distinguishing each role from the other, it does not try to be all encompassing but rather to encourage the reader to consider and reflect on what it means to advise or inspect.

To give context, the advisory work perspective makes use of the definition used by the Association of Education Advisers (AoEA). A sample of inspection jurisdictions, on the other hand, reflects the multifarious nature of differing regimes; those in the Netherlands, Northern Ireland, England and Sweden hopefully demonstrate this. These provide the reader with a context from which to generate thought and discussion.

What do we mean by inspection activity? Is it the same everywhere?

In many countries, inspection systems are embedded in government departments or as non-governmental department agencies, while others, such as Sweden, are completely independent.

In the Netherlands, the focus in their inspection frameworks is on 'school boards' as they provide a key leadership responsibility within the inspection process.

> *School governing boards are responsible for ensuring that the education provided in their schools is of satisfactory quality and that the financial administration meets requirements. The updated inspection framework (2021) encourages school governing boards even more emphatically to reflect on their own ambitions. Once every four years, the Inspectorate of Education carries out a 'Four-Yearly Inspection of School Governing Board and Schools' for every school governing board, which relates to the extent to which a school governing board takes responsibility and whether its schools meet quality requirements.*
> (Inspectorate of Education, The Netherlands, 2021)

In England, the Office for Standards in Education, Children's Services and Skills (Ofsted) states that '*Inspection provides independent, external evaluation and identifies what needs to improve in order for provision to be good or better*' (Ofsted, 2023).

In Northern Ireland, the Education and Training Inspectorate (2017) states that inspectors collect evidence to '*provide an unbiased, independent, professional assessment of the quality of learning and teaching, including the standards achieved by learners'.*

In Sweden, similarly, inspection is about helping to make sure that educational provision is of a high standard.

> *The primary objective of school inspections in Sweden is to ensure that schools provide high-quality education and comply with national regulations and standards.*
> (Swedish Schools Inspectorate (Skolinspektionen), 2021)

The following quotation from Croner-i (2023) seems to capture the essence of most inspection activity:

> *Inspection provides an independent, external evaluation of the quality of provision and standards achieved in a school, and a diagnosis of what it should do to improve, based upon a range of evidence. It ensures a measure of accountability and promotes the improvement of individual schools and the education system as a whole.*

The purpose of advisory work and what advisers do

The working definition used by members of the AoEA Development Team, compiled in 2020, is clear that *'every school, college and education provider has access to high-quality support, advice and challenge, which is independent and focused on improving outcomes for children, schools and their communities'*.

The AoEA considers that school advisers work within a specific context; the remit of their work is not governed by an inspection framework or handbook but on the transactional agreement with the school. Each agreement is unique to the organisation and requires what is termed by the AoEA as a 'Frame of Reference', which shows the range, scope and expectations of the adviser's engagement.

Distinguishing between the role of the inspector and education adviser

Table 2.1 assists in providing an 'at a glance' summary and distinction between the two roles.

Table 2.1 Inspector or adviser: what do each do?

Inspector	Adviser
Operates with legislative authority. Inspectors work within a legislative framework. In maintained schools and academies in England, for example, this is under section 5 of the Education Act 2005 and similar legislation in other jurisdictions.	Operates according to a **transactional agreement** (TA) with the organisation. The TA is key to good advisory work – defining the scope of the work, based upon a clear understanding of cause and effect in the school's performance.
Inspectors are accredited and trained by the inspection authority.	Advisers require professional credibility accrued from their work in delivering high-quality advice backed up with some form of accreditation, such as the AoEA.
Acts in accordance with an inspection framework.	Acts in relation to TA parameters agreed with the organisation.
Inspection findings are mostly published in line with protocols and made available widely and, in the case of England, the UK and a number of other jurisdictions, made public.	Findings are presented to the employing organisation in line with transactionally agreed protocols.
A report's findings are intended to provide a basis to help the school focus on areas where improvement is required the most.	A report's findings focus directly on the areas for improvement defined in the TA.

→

Table 2.1 (Cont.)

Inspection outcomes	Transactional outcomes
Provide summary judgements about a school's performance and within the UK models, currently separated out to show strengths and areas to improve.	The adviser's findings will be directly related to the aims of the adviser's work in the TA framework (school specific).

In summary, the inspector:

- has legislative authority to carry out an inspection using a specific framework;
- is accredited and trained by the inspection authority;
- reports their findings according to a specified template and timeline;
- identifies strengths and areas for improvement;
- provides reports that are mostly published to the institution and the public;
- provides report findings that may form the basis of subsequent inspection activity.

In summary, for the adviser (using the AoEA definition)

The transactional agreement between the adviser and the educational institution frames the context for their work:

- the TA defines, what the AoEA terminology refers to as the 'frame of reference' – the unique context of the school and the scope and expectations of the adviser's contribution;
- the TA states the parameters of the adviser's work, including the expectations of what will be achieved and the relevant accountability mechanisms;

- the TA shows the skills, knowledge, expertise and experience required to support school improvement;
- progress and outcomes are provided to the employing organisation in line with the transactionally agreed protocols;
- the organisation's leadership determines how widely reports are circulated.

Overlapping skill sets

Inspectors and advisers have experience from a variety of roles within and beyond the educational sector. They bring this experience and expertise to bear on their respective remits. Inspectors are trained under whatever jurisdiction they are working within and while advisers may also have experienced training of this kind, they deploy the range of skills that are specific to the TA. Their work is governed by the TA with the school. Inspectors meanwhile will deploy their skills and expertise in the application of each jurisdiction's inspection framework.

Whether inspector or adviser, the focus is the same – to contribute to improvement. Therefore, both roles require similar skill sets of being able to collect, collate, analyse and present information in a coherent and insightful way, which helps a school's leadership focus on improvement.

Shared skill sets

Both inspectors and advisers require the skill sets to undertake the following.

- Collect and analyse information, whether that be quantitative or qualitative.
- Understand cause and effect in relation to a school's performance.

- Recognise where capacity exists that can support improvement, defining clearly where that needs to be developed or acquired.

- While the inspector will be trained and accredited by the inspecting authority, an adviser's 'authority' may vary. The AoEA places great store on the adviser's credibility and self-effacing honesty when they agree to work with any institution. The AoEA's accreditation is sought by an increasing number of professionals working to support schools and colleges, enabling them to demonstrate their capacity to carry out advisory work.

- Honesty and integrity will guide an adviser's and inspector's commitment to working with an organisation by giving an assurance that they have the skills, knowledge, expertise and experience to undertake their work. As an adviser, being a generalist is not enough if the school requires particular expertise in, for example, Key Stage 4 mathematics or whole school reading. It is in no one's interest to take on a body of work where the skill set of the adviser doesn't match.

Conclusion

This chapter has demonstrated the distinctive nature of the role of the education adviser and that of the school or college inspector, as well as drawing attention to the skills they both share. However, there is sometimes ambiguity in the work that some advisers are asked to undertake. On the face of it, inspectors 'inspect' and advisers 'advise'. Yet take a recent request put to Anne, a colleague of mine, who was asked to carry out a 'mini pre-inspection' before a formal inspection took place. The headteacher wanted to know if the school would be 'inspection ready' and whether or not they would secure a 'good' judgement. She wanted reassurance that the school 'would be okay'. Was my colleague being asked to undertake advisory work or to conduct an inspectorial task? Another colleague was asked to undertake a 'safeguarding check' ahead of inspection. Again, is this advisory work or an inspectorial task? Does it matter if the focus is on helping the school to improve? The debate continues.

References

Croner-i (2023) Education Inspection Framework. [online] Available at: https://app.croneri.co.uk/topics/education-inspection-framework/summary (accessed 3 February 2024).

Education Act (2005). [online] Available at: www.legislation.gov.uk/ukpga/2005/18/contents (accessed 3 February 2024).

Education and Training Inspectorate, Northern Ireland (2017) The Inspection and Self-Evaluation Framework (ISEF). [online] Available at: www.etini.gov.uk/articles/inspection-and-self-evaluation-framework-isef (accessed 3 February 2024).

Inspectorate of Education, The Netherlands (2021) The 2021 Inspection Frameworks. [online] Available at: https://english.onderwijsinspectie.nl/inspection/inspection-of-schools-by-the-dutch-inspectorate-of-education/the-2021-inspection-frameworks (accessed 3 February 2024).

Office for Standards in Education in England (Ofsted) (2019, last updated in July 2023) Education Inspection Framework. [online] Available at: www.gov.uk/government/publications/education-inspection-framework (accessed 3 February 2024).

Swedish Schools Inspectorate (Skolinspektionen) (2021) About the Swedish Schools Inspectorate. [online] Available at: www.skolinspektionen.se/other-languages/english-engelska (accessed 3 February 2024).

3 Professional credibility: the attributes and skills of the education adviser

KEVIN MCDERMID

Key learning

- There should be a focus on developing and sustaining a strong track record of impact.

- It is important to demonstrate authority and professional credibility with clients.

- Education advisers are required to exhibit a wide range of distinct personal attributes and skills.

AoEA criteria

- Criterion 1. Demonstrating personal attributes and skills.

- Criterion 2. Ability to challenge and work within agreed protocols.

- Criterion 3. Acting as an enabler by providing support to drive delivery.

- Criterion 5. Demonstrating authority and professional credibility with clients.

Introduction

In this chapter, I reflect on my own experience of two national school improvement programmes in England and explore how, within the Association of Education Advisers we built, in part, on the lessons of those programmes to formulate what we came to identify as the essential skills and attributes that underpin the crucial role of the education adviser.

School Improvement Partners and National Challenge: a historical perspective

In 2008, the UK government of the day implemented an extensive, well-intentioned and well-funded centralised programme of school improvement across England called the National Challenge – it was targeted at all those secondary schools in the country where attainment in public examinations at age 16 fell below a certain threshold. At the highly publicised political launch of the programme, the Secretary of State for Education referred to those schools involved as '*failing schools*', a term which was picked up gleefully by certain sections of the national press. He also spoke about the threat of school closure or the '*structural solution*' of academisation, if the imposed attainment targets were not met.

Unsurprisingly, the great majority of the schools that had thus been 'named and shamed' served many of the most disadvantaged communities in the country, where students' attainment on entry to the school at age 11 or 14 was well below national averages; a significant number had been identified as good schools through the national inspection regime, Ofsted. Inspection reports at that time differentiated properly between attainment (students' raw scores on tests) and progress (the distance travelled from students' starting points), but this distinction was lost in the popular press' feeding frenzy.

Against this background, therefore, I had been invited, as a qualified National Challenge Adviser, by the Director of Education of a local authority in the north-east of England, the region with the lowest attainment in the country, to attend a meeting with the headteachers of the three schools in her jurisdiction that had been publicly identified as 'failing'. The Director had decided that she wanted to commission a single National Challenge Adviser (NCA) to work in her three nominated schools, so this was, in effect, my interview for that post. My brief was: '*Convince us that you have the skills, the knowledge and the experience to support us and help us to improve.*'

The ensuing interview was demanding – I remember this as one of the most challenging hours in my whole career in education spanning over 40 years. Even though I had the NCA 'badge', that alone was not going to cut much ice with these colleagues. In effect, I was being rigorously, and properly, challenged to demonstrate my professional credibility to a group of potentially resentful and suspicious headteachers. In such circumstances, one's own educational curriculum vitae (CV) is a crucial factor in establishing that credibility.

The adviser's CV: demonstrating a track record of successful impact in a similar setting

Having served successfully as a principal for over ten years in two inner-city comprehensive schools and a sixth form college in the north-east of England, I moved on to full-time school improvement advisory work in 2008, first as a School Improvement Partner (SIP) across three local authority areas. Like National Challenge, the SIP programme was a centrally funded, nationally directed initiative that was introduced in 2005 as an integral part of the government's 'New Relationship with Schools' and its 'National Strategies School Improvement Framework'. Every school in the country was required to have a SIP and it had been my good fortune in my own headships to have been assigned a highly effective colleague in that role. I learned a great deal from him about advisory skills and developed an appreciation that leadership and advisory skills, while they may overlap, are both complementary and discrete.

In order to qualify first as a SIP, and subsequently as an NCA, one had to submit a comprehensive online application and undergo a rigorous, competitive selection process over two days, involving a barrage of written, analytical and practical tasks, including role play. Once accredited, as participants in a national programme, working in local authority or regionally based teams, SIPs and NCAs benefitted hugely from regular high-quality professional learning and appraisal. The accreditations themselves, therefore, were a further factor in proving one's credibility to work in this field.

In my own extensive experience as a SIP, I had the privilege of working for the most part in schools in challenging circumstances, alongside a range of gifted, committed and resilient headteachers, principals, leaders, teachers and governors. In the same way as in my own headship days I had welcomed the support and challenge of an excellent SIP, I quickly discerned that what my school-based colleagues were principally seeking from me was fair, clear and honest moderation of their self-evaluation regarding the quality of education in their schools.

During that period, the school inspection framework was accompanied by a substantial body of data, running to over 100 pages, on every aspect of a school's relative performance, from attendance and exclusions to detailed analysis of student progress in every subject across the curriculum. Part of the SIP's role involved supporting the leadership of the school, including the governing board, in the interpretation of this data and in applying their analysis to ensure the school's self-evaluation was accurate and that its priorities for improvement were appropriate and well founded. The SIP was also commissioned to support the governing board in conducting the annual performance management of the headteacher.

However, despite some compelling evidence of impact of both the SIP and the NCA programmes on improving the quality of leadership in schools and raising the achievement of students, as confirmed by independent evaluations conducted by York Consulting in 2010 and 2011, following a change of national government both programmes were subsequently dissolved.

Furthermore, from 2010 onwards, local authorities across the country were subjected to a tight budgetary squeeze from central government, which led to a major reduction in their capacity to sustain school improvement teams beyond the statutory minimum oversight of special educational needs and safeguarding. Alongside the atomisation of the education system nationally that resulted from many schools opting out of local authority control to become independent state-funded academies, the school improvement 'market' changed radically, and a range of external providers emerged, including from not only large private sector organisations but also independent advisers, often operating as sole traders. How could schools know whether they might be dealing with snake oil salesmen?

The AoEA and demonstrating authoritative influence

In response to these trends, the Association of Education Advisers (AoEA) was formed in 2016 as an independent, not-for-profit organisation. In the Development Group, which comprised a number of experienced professionals from a broad range of roles in education and school improvement, we reasoned that, while professional standards exist for headteachers and inspectors, which, indeed, are often linked to compulsory qualifications at post-graduate level, nothing similar existed at that time for those professionals working as educational advisers or school improvement professionals.

It was also our contention that, in a Venn diagram of leadership, inspection and advisory skills and knowledge, while there is inevitably some overlap, there is also a distinct set of skills that are specific to the role of the school improvement professional.

Figure 3.1 Overlapping skill sets

Moreover, while the role of the principal or the inspector is enshrined in their statutory functions, the credibility of the education adviser in their crucial role depends for the most part on what we in the AoEA term their '*authoritative influence*'.

The distinct attributes and skills of the education adviser

In the AoEA Development Group we worked on defining and rationalising what we saw as the key qualities and knowledge that would enable an adviser to exert this authoritative influence; we settled on the following essential attributes for our 'person specification':

- has an impressive track record of effective and successful impact in a similar setting;
- has a credible professional presence when facing clients or presenting to large groups;
- is able to create and sustain an ethos of mutual respect with all stakeholders;
- has extensive knowledge of current and emerging educational legislation, policy and strategy;
- keeps abreast of research-based evidence about effective educational practice and demonstrates a real commitment to their own professional learning;
- knows where best practice is to be found, both locally and nationally, and is able to draw on that practice for the benefit of the educational setting;
- is fully conversant with the framework of educational accountability, including inspection, and can communicate its features effectively with the full range of stakeholders.

As we tested the above attributes with our pilot cohorts, we further rationalised the key skills that underpin the AoEA criteria for Associate accreditation as follows:

- works to clear and agreed protocols with regard to confidentiality;
- challenges performance in an objective but empathetic manner;
- addresses performance concerns resolutely, fairly and promptly;
- gives clear and honest feedback both verbally and in writing;
- develops and maintains positive relationships with staff at all levels of the organisation.

What firmly differentiates the skill set of the adviser from that of the inspector is the part that advisers play in the ongoing longitudinal journey of improvement within educational settings, providing professional support through:

- mentoring;
- performance management;
- coaching;
- training;
- providing ongoing advice;
- giving constructive criticism;
- motivating;
- persuading.

Conclusion

Just a word of caution in relation to the adviser's role. While the concept of the 'hero headteacher' has largely and rightly been discredited, in the AoEA we equally reject the idea of the 'hero adviser'. Several of the above functions, such as coaching, require specific training – we believe that professional credibility grows equally from a recognition that one individual may not be the best person to deliver that aspect of support. Having recognised that, the credible adviser knows that they can call on the specialist services that are available, for example, among the hundreds of Associates that have now been accredited through the AoEA.

4 The artful use of interpersonal skills to establish professional credibility and achieve maximum impact

EITHNE LEMING

Key learning

- *'The meaning of communication is the response that you get'* – a presupposition taken from neuro-linguistic programming (a branch of success psychology), which focuses attention on the importance of effective interpersonal skills and emphasises one's own responsibility for the outcome achieved in any communication.

- Beliefs about self shape our perceptions: our view of the world shapes our communication and also our view of situations, including the possibilities for change. The ability to identify and manage these in self and others can either act as a facilitator or barrier to the success or otherwise of a project.

- Contracting and project management skills: effective listening and questioning skills enable advisers to gain clarity of the brief. Also required is a high level of self-awareness in our own personal attributes to enable us to assess our suitability for achieving the requirements of the project.

AoEA criteria

- Criterion 1. Demonstrating personal attributes and skills.

- Criterion 2. Ability to challenge and work within agreed protocols.

- Criterion 3. Acting as an enabler by providing support to drive delivery.

- Criterion 5. Demonstrating authority and professional credibility with clients.

Introduction

> *Change comes more from managing the journey than from announcing the destination.*
>
> (William Bridges, 1991)

The AoEA criteria which form the particular focus for this chapter include:

- demonstrating personal attributes including interpersonal and communication skills and showing commitment (1.1, 1.2 and 1.3);
- authority and credibility: demonstrating authority and professional credibility with clients (5.1, 5.2, 5.3).

The case study presented here is a composite of several investigations I have undertaken over a period of several years. Any resemblance therefore to a particular school or indeed any individual is entirely coincidental so, for the purposes of this chapter, this commission was awarded by a governing body of a maintained school. It has been written to help illustrate the ways that these AoEA criteria can be demonstrated in advisory work.

Typically, the work of an investigator tends to fall into two distinct data-gathering aspects: first, a systematic review of certain documentary evidence; second, interviews to elicit the perceptions and views of individuals about certain events and situations. Analysis of the interviews in particular then involves making sense of the resulting complex mix of psychological, emotional and social aspects of communication, all of which affect the culture and climate of the school; this is an especially fascinating area of work.

Context

The school in this particular case (school C) had been created by the amalgamation, two years previously, of two relatively small primary schools in adjoining villages serving a rural community. A headteacher from one of the schools (school A) was appointed to the newly formed primary school upon the retirement of the headteacher of the second school (school B). The governing body of the amalgamated school included some governors from both former schools plus some recently appointed representatives. The recently appointed chair of governors and the vice chair were both experienced governors who had joined the governing body of school A prior to amalgamation.

I was contacted about the commission as a result of recommendations made by local authority colleagues.

The information-gathering stage

Initially, this stage proved complex since only the very sketchiest of details were provided in writing about the brief by governors who were anxious to protect the anonymity of the school and maintain confidentiality at this stage. This meant that a fair degree of active and reflective listening was required in order to enable the governors to explain their perspective on the issues.

I learned that the situation had been complicated by a division within the governing body that had developed along the 'fault lines' of the previous schools, which had caused the first complaints received from staff to be ignored by the previous chair. This had led to both a delay in formally responding to these complaints and an escalation in the range and degree of these, which resulted in some allegations being sent to the local authority, Ofsted and the Standards and Testing Agency.

Although no specific details were provided about the complaints, indications at this point were that complaints were wide-ranging and included allegations of headteacher misconduct regarding elements of staffing and finance, maladministration of SATs, plus an acrimonious breakdown in relationships between two staff members (from school B) and the headteacher. It remained a challenge, therefore, to establish what the exact scope and the nature of the enquiry would be.

Establishing professional credibility and contracting

During an interview with the chair and vice chair of governors, I had an opportunity to test out whether this was a commission that matched my expertise. I began by stating what I would *not* be able to offer; for example, if they required an HR, finance or safeguarding specialist, then I was not the right person to appoint. This is typically an approach I adopt to both demonstrate commitment to ensuring the success of the commission and, importantly, to show integrity.

I outlined my relevant experience, particularly that which I gained investigating allegations of maladministration of SATs on behalf of the Standards and Testing Agency. Since there is a protocol for these kinds of investigations which is always directed by the Standards and Testing Agency, I stated clearly that I would *not* be able to investigate those particular complaints. I then went on to outline what I *could* offer by observing that, in my experience of investigating allegations of maladministration of tests, this was never an isolated issue of process and procedure. Instead, often these allegations were accompanied by underlying conflicts relating to leadership of the ethos, culture and climate within the school. These more qualitative and relational aspects were ones for which I possessed the relevant knowledge, skills and experience to investigate.

I checked the scope of the commission, particularly whether they were aware of any other complainants likely to come forward (they were not aware of any others). Then in relation to the well-being of the headteacher, it was important to identify whether he was already aware of the proposed investigation and his reaction to this.

Although I was now in possession of all the details of the brief and discussion indicated that the panel wanted me to undertake the work, at no point had it been expressly stated this was the case. Therefore, I checked this directly, including their understanding of what I had offered by asking: '*What confirms to you that I am the right person to undertake this commission?*' Once it became clear that their reasons matched with my expertise and proposal, the commission was accepted.

The chair of governors provided necessary documentation such as a 'Terms of Reference' document, copies of the original written complaints, plus contact details for the complainants. A set of questions was then agreed with the chair of governors. At this point I was also advised that one complainant (a teacher) had resigned with effect from the end of the previous term and the other (a member of the support staff) had resigned the previous week, citing a lack of action to the original complaints submission and therefore a loss of trust in the governing body.

Setting expectations, managing beliefs and perceptions

My interview invitation written by email to both complainants was designed to establish a degree of trust in the process and confidence in me as an 'independent' investigator. Whenever there is a risk of barriers to the success of a project being created by certain unhelpful sets of beliefs and perceptions held by participants, gaining the trust of participants can present a significant challenge.

In such situations, I give careful thought to establishing rapport and to do this I frequently begin with a set of 'truisms'. Normally I use at least three statements which are indisputable facts. The technique works by eliciting three metaphorical (or actual) nods of the head in agreement. This ensures a degree of 'matching' which encourages engagement and begins to build trust. Examples used in this case were as follows:

> *I have been passed your name and contact details by {name}, the chair of governors of {name of school}, in relation to a complaint that you made on {date}, where I understand that you were until {date} employed at the school as a {role}.*

My introduction then aimed to demonstrate my independence (a stated concern of the complainants) and my suitability for the work, so this included my name and a few relevant details of my experience, both locally working in the local authority and at some other local schools.

I then outlined the interview process. Options included either a telephone or virtual meeting along with various dates and times. This was a deliberate strategy since a 'limited choice' ensures it is manageable for me but importantly offers a degree of control for the complainants. This is psychologically supportive for engaging participants in situations where the balance of power and control, or especially feelings of the lack of it, may potentially be powerful inhibitors.

Establishing professional credibility

Building the trust and confidence of participants in the process was a key focus for the beginning of each interview, so I set out to try to reassure them about the record taking and the boundaries of the investigation. I explained that I had a set of questions based on what I had read of their initial written complaints, that I would type contemporaneous notes while they spoke and that a copy of these notes would then be supplied for checking with them so that a final version was agreed with them. I also assured them that full transcripts would not be sent to the whole governing body (something agreed with the chair) since there was concern that the previous chair in particular had not acted as required when the first complaints were made. The full governing body would have access to the report on my findings and any recommendations made.

Once these interviews with complainants had been completed I discovered, however, that more complainants were now beginning to emerge. Apparently, feeling reassured by the process established and the relayed experiences of the two recently interviewed complainants, another seven complainants emerged. None were in fact currently employed at the school, having resigned over recent months since the appointment of the headteacher. The commission had grown exponentially and a return to contracting was needed!

> *The world as we see it is only the world as we see it. Others may see it differently.*
>
> (Albert Einstein, nd)

Figure 4.1 helps to illustrate how individuals may perceive things differently.

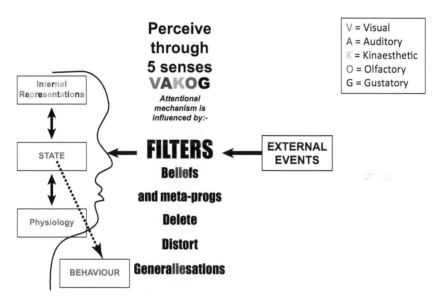

Figure 4.1 'Our perceptions can be very different'
Source: Kathryn Temple, The Life Long Learning Company

My method of analysis was to group the qualitative themes that emerged from the interviews of complainants. In total I identified nine themes and grouped these according to frequency in a table using illustrative quoted phrases as headings. Three themes identified appeared at a particularly high level of frequency across all complainants, but in any case the remaining six also pointed to areas of concern regarding the leadership of school, culture, climate, ethos and a perceived lack of positive, respectful and professional relationships.

Documentation was also reviewed, including email correspondence sent to staff from the headteacher, various notes taken at meetings and various policies such as staff appraisal, staff well-being and staff code of conduct. The nine themes were used to formulate and agree questions for the headteacher and notably to identify any alleged variance in practice from the stated policies. A check was again made with the chair regarding the well-being of the head before contact was made to arrange an interview.

Success again rested on my ability, at the first point of contact with the headteacher, to establish a level of trust and confidence in the process and in my own ability to remain a fair and independent investigator, particularly in a situation where the headteacher had been under some considerable pressure for quite some time. Again, I followed the same process for agreeing the record of the interview and the headteacher responded with his own particular thanks for my approach.

The report was written with findings and recommendations cross-referenced to the relevant staff policies and the headteachers' standards document (Department for Education, 2020), particularly in relation to the following standards:

> *Establish and sustain the school's ethos and strategic direction in partnership with those responsible for governance and through consultation with the school community.*
>
> *Promote positive and respectful relationships across the school community and a safe, orderly and inclusive environment.*

The importance of referencing findings and recommendations to national or statutory guidance supports one's own professional credibility but also draws attention away from the potential for unhelpfully subjective and emotionally charged judgements (or at least the perception of these by those reading the report) and allows for a more objective consideration of findings and recommendations.

The meaning of the communication is the result that you get

In conversations with both the headteacher and the chair of governors I also wanted to help them reflect upon organisational stress (caused by external events such as an amalgamation) and the effect it can have on staff teams and relationships. My observation to them was that dysfunctional and destructive staff relationship issues are not necessarily the result of any intentional or 'conscious' miscommunication. In a further attempt to depersonalise a highly emotionally charged situation by way of creating additional objectivity and insight to the situation, I referenced a publication by the Tavistock Institute; *The Unconscious at Work: Individual and Organizational Stress in the Human Services* (Obholzer and Zagier Roberts, 1994). This is a collection of case studies about how when human services such as health, education and social care become dysfunctional (often due to external pressures), this can manifest itself unhelpfully in the relationships of those working within them. Individuals or groups within the staff team can, in such circumstances, either become the unwitting 'unconscious' receptacles of negative emotions or the 'unconscious' projectors of the organisational stress through their communication with others; those working in human services appear to be more at risk of these issues.

Referencing a publication written by members of a highly respected national body in the field of organisational psychology also provided some additional credibility to support findings of an investigation where the issues at play were predominantly individuals' subjective emotional and psychosocial responses and perceptions. Ultimately though, whether intentional or not, responsibility for the 'result' of any miscommunication has to be acknowledged and accepted in order to repair relationships and move forward. In the setting of a school, since the climate and ethos are the responsibility of the leadership of that school, where change is needed it has to begin with the headteacher and governors, and as a result my report and its recommendations reflected this reality.

 Further reading

Terry, R and Churches, R (2009) *The NLP Toolkit: For Teachers, Trainers and School Leaders*. Carmarthen: Crown Publishing Ltd.

References

Bridges, W (1991) *Managing Transitions*. USA: William Bridges and Associates Inc.

Department for Education (2020) *Headteachers' Standards 2020*. [online] Available at: www.gov.uk/government/publications/national-standards-of-excellence-for-headteachers/headteachers-standards-2020 (accessed 3 February 2024).

Einstein, A (nd) Top 500 Albert Einstein Quotes. [online] Available at: https://quotefancy.com (accessed 15 March 2024).

Obholzer, A and Zagier Roberts, V (eds) (1994) *The Unconscious at Work: Individual and Organisational Stress in the Human Services*. Written by the members of the Tavistock Clinic Consulting to Institutions Workshop. Reprinted 2002/2003. London: Routledge.

Temple, K (nd) Success Psychologist, The Life Long Learning Company. [online] Available at: www.lifelonglearningcompany.com (accessed 3 February 2024).

5 Influential report writing: communicating with accuracy, clarity and transparency

MARTYN BEALES

Key learning

- Reports from inspectors will be different from those created by advisers. The lack of a legislative framework can be liberating but creates challenge for the adviser.

- A report can only be as good as the quality of the activity undertaken to gather the required information. The adviser should ensure that the purpose and audience of the report are established prior to school-based activity.

- There are a number of traps that the adviser should be aware of when writing a report. These should be considered carefully in order that they can be avoided and an effective report produced that adds value for the school.

AoEA criteria

- Criterion 2. Ability to challenge and work within agreed protocols.

- Criterion 3. Acting as an enabler by providing support to drive delivery.

- Criterion 5. Demonstrating authority and professional credibility with clients

- Criterion 7. Providing clear, insightful and well-written reports.

Introduction

As a general inspector/adviser and school improvement manager for over 50 schools, I have written and quality assured a wide range of reports for local authorities and multi-academy trusts over a number of years. In this chapter, I would like to consider the conditions that need to be in place for a report to 'land' successfully, both for the commissioner and the adviser.

The advisory visit and the subsequent report are inextricably linked. It is difficult to write an effective report if there is a lack of clarity in relation to:

- who is commissioning the report, who it is for and how it will be used;
- the 'terms of reference' to guide the way the report is focused.

There are important differences in the nature of advisory reports and inspection reports. A report from a regulatory inspector, as explored in more detail in Chapter 2, is likely to be tightly linked to a statutory or similarly established framework. For example, Ofsted reports are determined by a specific and published legislative brief. Although not all will agree on what is included in such a framework, it is widely available and accessible. In contrast, a report from an adviser is not likely to be tightly written against such a regulatory framework even if it forms part of the context for the visit. While this brings greater freedom and flexibility, it also creates a challenge for the adviser in that the 'rules of the game' may not be as clear.

The commissioning

Reports can be commissioned for a variety of reasons. The adviser needs to appreciate that a commissioner may have a particular agenda that they are seeking to pursue, and that this may result in them wanting to determine or dictate the tone of the report and what is recorded. The commissioners, whether leaders of a school, or the trust, governors or local authority, may be expecting a report that affirms their view or to dig deeper into an issue or challenge. The evidence of the visit may or may not affirm the existing evaluative view of the commissioner in relation to an aspect of school performance and the factors of most significance. Professional credibility is an essential aspect of the role of the adviser; we must ensure that what is recorded within any report can be evidenced through the activities undertaken as part of the visit.

The role of the adviser is to shape a brief that is known and understood by all parties – the client, the commissioner and the adviser *in advance of the visit*. The adviser will want to ensure that all parties are aware of what is being explored and, as importantly, what is not, in order that the report meets the brief and is professionally received. An adviser cannot know in advance what will need to be reported so must take care not to create misleading expectations that the report will be an affirmation or a highly challenging critique. This is particularly the case when a visit and report is being externally commissioned.

School leaders will have a 'lived and breathed' experience of visits from external advisers or inspectors. Some of this experience will be highly positive, some less so. Ensuring that there is transparency in relation to the purpose of the visit, and the way in which the subsequent report will and, sometimes more importantly, won't be used will help the adviser to build an effective working relationship with school leaders; this undoubtedly supports the adviser in writing an effective report.

Common report-writing mistakes

There are a number of traps that should be avoided when writing the report. The adviser might consider these risks in advance of the visit, in order that they remain disciplined in their focus and gather the key information that they need to write an effective report. These are as follows.

- Including absolutely everything in the report that was undertaken within the visit.

- Feeling an affinity or sympathy for the school leader and so reporting what was said without critical reflection and objectivity.

- Overstating the significance of limited evidence – *I saw it so it must always be true.*

- Obscuring the critical messages of a report to the leaders and other audiences that need clarity.

- Including content in the report that was not fully explored with leaders at the time of the visit.

- Writing too many actions or writing actions without reference to the capacity that exists, or which needs to be developed to achieve them, or without reference to the timescales required.

Effective report-writing skills

Being evaluative

There is a danger that a report merely becomes a description of all of the activity undertaken during the visit – a chronological narrative. The adviser may feel the need to demonstrate that they worked hard on the day by including everything. They may feel that the commissioner needs to see value for money in terms of the volume of the report. The risk here is that the 'nuggets' of real value become lost within a sea of words. A short bullet-pointed list can be helpful in clarifying what was done, but the report must be selective and evaluative if it is to add value to the thinking of leaders in the school.

A report can become a document that simply describes what the senior leaders tell you about their school. As an adviser, it is important that the report takes account of the views of senior leaders but this must be set alongside other information that has been considered by the adviser. Reports can soon become a series of statements prefaced by phrases such as '*The headteacher reported that* ...' or '*It is the view of the SENDCo that* ...'. The report should seek to confirm any assertions made by leaders through connecting these statements to evidence gathered externally or through activities undertaken on the day. It should not simply be an account of views; otherwise, commissioners could rightly complain that they can't see the point of the adviser visiting if they are simply reporting what was already known about the school.

Capturing evidence

In order to be transparent to the audience, the report should include some tangible examples of what has been seen so that leaders can 'see' and 'feel' their school within the report. The report must capture the specifics of that moment in time. The adviser should appreciate that, while they will have worked hard to establish an effective working relationship with the school leader, they must remain objective if they are to report with honesty, clarity and transparency. More difficult and challenging messages need to be given unequivocally and be evidence informed but delivered sensitively and with an appreciation that it is the school leaders who will need the clarity and energy for further improvement.

Being cautious and careful not to leap to conclusions

Reporting what is seen on the day of the visit as the whole and only truth can be unhelpful. Of course, this is a feature of inspection reporting due to the episodic nature of the event and the expectations of judgement against a framework. As an adviser, it is understandable that school leaders will want you to capture their school on a 'best day'. The adviser must anticipate that this may be the case because there is a danger that an overly optimistic or generous view of the school is presented through the report. The same is true, of course, of overly critical evaluation based on slight evidence. Sources of evidence cannot be entirely ignored, but the report must demonstrate that the adviser has sought to draw upon a range of information when arriving at an evaluation. The adviser should be cautious about presenting information gathered through a single activity or short time in class as absolute fact; this may come back to bite them further down the line and may impact upon professional credibility. Instead, consider identifying such evidence as pointing to the importance of further review or additional evidence gathering. Take care to write proportionately about both improvement issues and successes. Consider adding value to thinking rather than making a summative, evaluative judgement unless this is overwhelmingly clear. Lastly, wherever possible, write in the present tense; evaluations are about how things currently present.

Making the key messages clear

The skill of the adviser is to craft a report that enables the audience to understand the key messages being delivered. When reviewing reports, I read the first line of each paragraph within a report. This enables me to get a sense of whether the adviser has captured the strengths of the school and the key areas that require development.

Often key messages can become buried within the paragraph, or the start of a paragraph presents a very different picture than the end of the paragraph. It is better that the adviser ensures that the key message is delivered in the first sentence of the paragraph, and that subsequent sentences clarify the evidence that has been drawn upon and the actions that leaders can take, as discussed with them.

The adviser must also consider how accessible the report is to the audience. School leaders may be very familiar with specific educational terminology but often other audiences may lack the understanding required to make sense of the report. The skill of the adviser is to take the complicated and messy nature of school improvement and make it accessible to the commissioner of the report through well-chosen evidence or examples.

Avoiding surprises

Leaders cannot be surprised by the report. During the report-writing process, the adviser may identify where they could have done things differently during the visit. For example, the adviser may wish to have explored a line of enquiry more fully with the school leader. Or it may occur to the adviser that they could have added to the thinking of the leader at a point during the visit. In these circumstances, the adviser cannot rewrite what actually happened or was discussed on the day; the report has to capture the reality of the visit if honesty, transparency and accuracy are to be maintained.

Conclusion

Where improvement is necessary, the report must provide the school (both the headteacher and the governors or trust body) with a clear and practical basis for action. Generally, if the report does not clarify what can be done to improve the school, its impact will be limited. Effective reports provide clear messages about actions that could be taken where improvement is necessary. The number of recommendations should be manageable and so the report should indicate which are the most important. The adviser will also need to make a judgement about leadership capacity and school context when determining action; in my current role we talk about 'what', not 'how', because headteachers have strategic autonomy. However, in some contexts the adviser may need to suggest a range of potential solutions to support the school leader's thinking, including how additional capacity might be developed. The adviser should also reflect with leaders on whether further external support would be helpful or necessary.

A key feature of the work of the adviser is to add value. The nature of the added value can take many forms. It can be a form of external validation or challenging school leaders' thinking in relation to a new initiative or response to an existing analysis of performance. If the visit, and the subsequent report, is to truly add value, the context must be agreed prior to the adviser undertaking the activities that will then inform the report. The report is a summary that marks a moment in time; it is the capturing of the advisory activity that has, in itself, added value to the school, written with accuracy, clarity and transparency.

6 The ability to challenge through supportive intervention

LES WALTON, CBE

Key learning

- The word 'challenge' can have unfortunate connotations and we should challenge the 'received wisdom' of what we mean by challenge.

- Supportive intervention works best when leaders invite challenge as a supportive process of continuous improvement.

- There needs to be absolute clarity in the terms of engagement underpinning the supportive intervention.

- Creating the conditions for a 'no blame', mutually supportive, working relationship between the adviser, the leader and those adults and students in the organisation lays the right foundations for a successful intervention and sustainable improvement.

AoEA criteria

- Criterion 1. Demonstrating personal attributes and skills.

- Criterion 2. Ability to challenge and work within agreed protocols.

- Criterion 3. Acting as an enabler by providing support to drive delivery.

- Criterion 5. Demonstrating authority and professional credibility with clients.

Introduction

Education advisers are often described as people who provide support and challenge to school leaders. It is, of course, important that we are able to support, challenge and enable our school and college leaders to lead effectively. There is often an inherent assumption when we consider the support and challenge role of the adviser that support is opposite to challenge, that those who challenge are coercive and directive, and that those who support are gentle and permissive. I want to challenge the received wisdom of what we mean by challenge, consider the role of the adviser as a supportive interventionist and how leaders, in turn, might seek to embrace and invite the challenge as a supportive process in continuously improving their school, college or system of schools.

Defining supportive intervention

Supportive intervention is based on the simple belief that people want to do a good job and that, even when people get it wrong, they do actually want to get it right. Therefore, it is a central role of the adviser to support leaders in the achievement of their objectives – a process that both the leader and the adviser buy in to. This approach focuses on enabling support and challenge without blame. The approach also requires humility from both the adviser and the leader since as a shared journey this process of supportive intervention enables both the adviser and the leader to learn from each other, assisting each other in bringing about even better improvement.

Shared common purpose and core beliefs

We should never lose sight of the fact that teachers choose to teach and leaders choose to lead because they want to make a positive difference in affecting the lives of the young people in their care. We work on the assumption that whatever the politics, the systems, the procedures and the practicalities that are in place, our children and young people are at the heart of everything we do. While on the rare occasion we may need to challenge those who deviate from this core purpose, the overwhelming majority share this belief and will work with their leaders to this end.

Enabling supportive intervention

Working to the principle that the central goal is a shared one, supportive intervention becomes about 'removing the blockages' from the system which prevent the well-motivated, able majority from achieving their full potential. These 'blockages' are more likely to be to do with systems, procedures and inadequate decision-making processes than a lack of personal ability, capacity or, indeed, desire to carry out a given role. Supportive intervention works best when:

- the leadership actually invites 'challenge';
- the intervention is needed and wanted by all parties – stakeholders, the leadership and governors;
- the critical friendship role is central, providing honest feedback but not instructing since any change for the better is informed by the evidence and shared understanding that it is needed.

There are, of course, occasions when assessment of risk requires the adviser to intervene without invitation. This should be a 'where all else has failed approach' or where, for example, the safety or safeguarding of others is of concern.

Terms of engagement

There needs to be absolute clarity about how the supportive intervention will work since this will assist in enabling mutual understanding and commitment from both the leader and the adviser. 'How' both will work together is as important as identifying 'what' will be done. In summary:

- supportive intervention should be based on clear, agreed statements and principles, allowing for any intent or proposed, resultant action to be checked against the values and principles that both the adviser and leader are signed up to;
- terms of engagement should state clearly how this will be of benefit to the children and young people;

- we should work on the development of the self-esteem of those with whom we work, which is essential in eradicating fear and in enabling everyone to achieve their full potential – in this sense we are 'person-centred' in all that we do in improving the quality of education for our children and young people;

- as advisers, we are 'positively optimistic' and solution focused, inspiring leaders to want to work with us in overcoming challenge and/or adversity.

Key mantra for the 'supportive interventionist'

No individual has all the answers

It is not appropriate for an adviser, or indeed leader, to present themselves as having all the answers. The role of the adviser is to assist those with whom they work in discovering these for themselves and, in so doing, for those in the organisation itself to develop improved ways of thinking and working. The supportive interventionist avoids analysis based on anecdote and individual bias; a systematic analysis should be based logically on data and intelligence with the information analysed systematically, undertaken in partnership with those who are being advised.

Success breeds success

I have been quoted as saying I would even '*celebrate grass growing*'. I am not ashamed of the belief that one should continually feed back success to young people and colleagues. It is important in offering supportive intervention to foster a sense of pride and strengthen the emotional resolve to want to do more and, in a wider context, develop those same positive relationships with the media so that the successes and in some cases the revival of organisations can be widely recognised and celebrated. No organisation is as good or as bad as its reputation: we should all strive to ensure that there is a balanced critical judgement and honest self-evaluation, in the best interests of all our children and young people. And recognising the successes and building on those are crucial in enabling greater success.

Foster a sense of fun and positivity

In a book entitled *The Divided School*, Peter Woods asserts that an organisation can be judged to be in difficultly when it has lost its sense of humour, its sense of fun. In enabling supportive intervention in an organisation, it is crucial to retain a sense of humour and develop a team spirit, so that team leadership is not focused on any one individual but on the belief that everyone in the team has the capacity to become the leader and lead in their own right. It is important to continually express positive expectations of colleagues within teams. Positive feedback should be honest, not patronising, and focused on what people can actually do as part of the collective endeavour.

Understand the context and make it stick

When working as a supportive interventionist in an organisation, some of the internal currents may not be immediately evident. There is always a need to understand the internal politics and people dynamics, especially those which are not readily visible. It is key that the adviser assists leaders in arriving at their own validation of their own work. In other words, it is not the adviser providing the supportive intervention who should see the need for or the resultant improvement but those who have the responsibility for leading it. In this way, when the adviser walks away, capacity is strengthened with leaders understanding their own accountability for bringing about their own sustainable improvement.

Conclusion

In keeping with the AoEA's core purpose of providing quality advice and support to schools and colleges, central to the adviser's role is enabling a positive climate for improvement, working with leaders and organisations who strive to create the learning environment where people want to work, make a difference and continuously improve. Supportive intervention should enable positive working relationships within both fit-for-purpose formal and informal structures. The adviser should assist leaders in shedding light on issues in a non-judgemental evidence-based way, working with leaders to bring about their own continuous and sustainable improvement.

For many years I have based my philosophy on three principal sources:

1. Carl Rogers' views about developing positive self-regard and allowing people to grow;

2. Perls' view that it is a group joining together which can create results greater than any individual's;

3. Maslow's belief that people need basic caring for and love, where in the work environment good working conditions and a positive climate for improvement lay the foundations for all to achieve.

As a supportive interventionist there is a fine balance to be struck between, at the one extreme interfering or becoming too involved, or at the other being too objective or too distant, in which case the organisation may feel you don't care or see you as part of the solution. In the end, the role of advisers is to be unnoticed when they move on: to be able to walk away from the organisation knowing that it will have evolved, and with leaders confident that they have the strengthened capacity to continue to grow professionally and improve the provision for their children and young people.

 References

Maslow, A H (1943) *A Theory of Human Motivation*. Ontario: York University.

Perls, F S (1951) *Gestalt Therapy: Excitement and Growth in the Human Personality*. Gouldsboro: The Gestalt Journal Press, Inc.

Rogers, C (1976) *Client-Centered Therapy: Its Current Practice, Implications and Theory*. London: Little Brown Book Group Ltd.

Woods, P (1979) *The Divided School*. London: Routledge.

7 Implementing continuous change: embracing the resistance

DR LOUIS DELORETO

Key learning

- When working as advisers, finding and embracing resistance allows us to keep the focus on what we can control.

- When we work constructively with colleagues, we can instil a sense of urgency for continuous change.

AoEA criteria

- Criterion 1. Demonstrating personal attributes and skills.

- Criterion 2. Ability to challenge and work within agreed protocols.

- Criterion 3. Acting as an enabler by providing support to drive delivery.

- Criterion 5. Demonstrating authority and professional credibility with clients.

Visual exemplification

As educators, it is our obligation to embrace the opportunity for school improvement we all share. However any significant area of school improvement is defined, it will involve a process that requires a change in the way we do things. This includes how we think about and approach change. Our conditioned response is to find ways to fix the deficits we see for students. In doing so, we often fail to recognise the possibility of systemic conditions that are contributing to undesirable student outcomes. The result is a cycle of failure in school reform.

One way to look at degrees of change is to imagine a person with their arm halfway extended in front of them with the forefinger extended.

If the person then moves their finger in a small clockwise motion making small circles in the air with the wrist and elbow staying in a fixed position, you can visualise a circle being repeated over and over. This represents a degree of change. Every time the finger motions to the right, that is progress. However, the motion quickly moves back to the left to complete the circle. This motion represents a return to the same point where the circle began. Drawing a circle repeatedly on a piece of paper will show the same effect.

What this visual can show us if we choose to look at it in the context of a successful change process is that the improvement is confined and does not move beyond the same circle. This is a phenomenon that is repeated in schools across the world. For example, an instructional practice is implemented and shows success in improved student outcomes in one classroom but does not make enough of an impact to move the entire school forward. This leads to disparities in educational experiences of children.

Now visualise the same starting point but the elbow and shoulder joints open up and the arm swings to the right as the finger makes the circle. Then the person begins stepping to the right to stay on pace with the arm motion and soon the whole body is moving in the same direction. The circle still comes back around to the left signifying the reality that it is nearly impossible to move an entire organisation without some setbacks; however, the difference is the overall movement in one direction. Again, if drawing on a piece of paper, the motion would look like continuous connecting loops moving from left to right on the page.

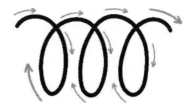

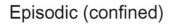

Episodic (confined)   Continuous (systemic)

Figure 7.1 Episodic versus continuous improvement

In both models, the circular motion of the finger is the same and we tend to gravitate to the right to be a part of the exciting prospect of progress. That part of the cycle that swings us to the left and backward is what we fear when we try to do something new or take a risk in an attempt to make improvements or address a problem. In this chapter, we focus on that part of the loop that swings us back to the left. In doing so, we embrace and explicitly address the resistance part of the change process. By validating resistance in all phases in a change process, we can move from one highly successful classroom to a guaranteed high-quality educational experience for all students.

Determining the root cause and discerning what we can and cannot influence

Resistance comes in many forms and is present in all phases of a substantive change process. While recognising resistance is important, embracing it as a key component in meeting the desired student outcomes is a mindset that requires both courage and resolve. There are several approaches to determining causes to problems. It is not difficult to find a root cause analysis protocol that will serve as a helpful tool in determining what problem or condition exists. If we were to use the example of low student performance, we could determine the root causes fairly quickly. Some of the causes would point to the factors beyond the control of the school such as poverty, which has been widely studied and accepted as a predictor of lower student performance. There will also be factors within the sphere of influence of a school such as high-leverage instructional strategies and effective tier II and III intervention strategies.

Separating out what we can control and focusing on these factors is the first step in embracing the resistance. This is where the continuous change mindset comes into play. Being clear about what we can address will provide the focus and direction necessary to maintain the movement forward (and to the right). After identifying the root causes, being honest and open about what we can and should do in order to make the desired change happen is an essential step in understanding the obstacles that can threaten our success. As advisers, our role is to facilitate this awareness of root causes in our clients in order to focus on strategies that are within our sphere of influence.

Understanding and embracing resistance to change

Let's revisit the different forms and levels of resistance present in a change scenario. Contrary to common belief, resistance is not always an intentional opposition to change. At the individual or personal level, resistance can be present, ranging from blatant refusal to participate in the change process to a genuine lack of understanding of the problem or what to do about it. To dismiss and categorise someone as 'a resistor' is to fall into the trap of creating an 'us versus them' dynamic which is counterproductive to our efforts. Recognising the presence of those who simply do not want to engage in the change process, we must decide when to let them go and not engage. For those who are hesitant or not fully committed, assuming positive intentions will get us further than approaching resistance as something we must combat. With this mindset, we can dive deeper into understanding the questions our colleagues have and address them directly and honestly. These may come in the form of wanting to see student performance data or research that explains the phenomenon we are attempting to address. A willingness to look behind the questions is another perspective worth exploring. Understanding that change can be perceived as a threat to one's social standing is important. For example, a successful teacher is now being asked to approach learning with the least successful students in mind, which will cause a shift in the way they approach their instruction. This is a significant change for the educator that can leave them feeling vulnerable. Another common example is the educator who is hesitant to engage due to a fear of conflict that often arises within a change process.

Resistance on an institutional level is also prevalent in school systems, particularly those school systems who view themselves as successful. Keeping in mind that a school and school district is made up of individuals, systemic or institutional resistance is really a collection of individual perceptions. This can be more dangerous, particularly when this resistance is organised and shows itself in the form of a collective body such as a parent group, the teachers' union or even board of education members. Although a more organised resistance can be intimidating, keeping the same perspective of opportunity is still the best way to approach change. If there is a visible opposition, you have successfully brought the resistance into the open and can now address their specific concerns like you have with the individual. Moving from the darkness to the light is, in fact, progress.

There is extensive research on resistance to change in organisations and in schools in particular. Developing a high level of cognition of all forms of resistance can prove useful as our understanding of the root causes to resistance is paramount in implementing continuous change. This will include an in-depth understanding of self-awareness and how even change agents can become resistors if biases are unrecognised through reflection and skills and knowledge are not developed through professional learning activities. Again, a threat to the success of any change process is inattentiveness to both the obvious and well-known systemic obstacles that exist but also those that pop up at different points in the process.

The call for change is so common in education that it can have the same effect as background noise heard in everyday life. It's there, we hear it, but we have other things to do right now. The immediacy of the tasks we have in front of us demands our attention and the routine keeps us busy. As advisers, it is our responsibility to maintain a sense of urgency and keep our clients from falling back into the cycle of daily routines. From a student perspective, they only have a finite amount of time to be prepared for their next phase in life after their K-12 educational experience. Any delays to the change process allows students to move on and not experience the benefits of improved instructional practice or a healthier school climate and culture.

A four-step process

The sense of urgency for those of us interested in making continuous change has to be cultivated and felt throughout a school or school system. To do this, there has to be an unwavering focus on *a four-step process*. The responsibility of the adviser is to instil in our clients the importance of moving through this progression to achieve the desired outcomes.

Step 1: the curiosity to look

Discrepancies in student participation and performance exist in all school systems. Disaggregating data by demographic groups (race, gender, socio-economic status, etc.) will show us where we need to focus our time and efforts. It will also allow us to ask our constituents why they believe these differences exist and what we think we can do about them.

Step 2: the confidence to share

Once we uncover the data, it is our obligation to make it known no matter what it reveals. Making public the different racial participation rates in academic and civic-minded organisations such as advanced courses or the national honour society will cause some discomfort when we apply the questions above to a current example involving our children. In publishing student outcome data, a school system is disclosing their intent to make improvements. With a new and improved student-focused mindset, however, it can be a freeing and liberating step towards the type of institutional and continuous change we are after.

Step 3: the courage to act

Now that we have made public the issues in need of our attention, our actions must connect with student outcomes. This requires being focused on how time is used in professional learning and dedicated towards actions that directly relate to improved student outcomes. In doing so, we will embrace accountability and a results mindset towards improved student outcomes.

Step 4: the resolve to 'hang on in there'

We have to fight through the resistance in order to adhere to our sense of urgency. Keeping in mind that the educational system is set up and works for those in power, any changes can and will be perceived as a threat to many stakeholders, including successful educators. Engaging these stakeholders as ambassadors to change will provide security and divide the work into manageable components for each individual contributing to the collective belief that truly is about the children and young people we serve.

Conclusion

As educational advisers, our obligation is to the students and families we serve. In keeping with this focus, our resolve has to be greater than the forces that work against our best efforts. This is a vital role in our pursuit of guaranteed high-quality learning outcomes for students and must be embraced.

8 Working in concert with a school's leadership team

ERIC HALTON

Key learning

- All schools, not just those subject to a form of intervention, benefit from high-quality external advice that actively builds co-constructed clarity about the priorities for improvement and how this might be achieved.

- Advisers skilfully use their previous experiences, achievements and professional knowledge but not as a template for others to follow since school leaders have the right and responsibility to make strategic choices.

- Joint and shared experiences with leaders during consultancy visits and effective listening and responding skills enable school leaders to gain new perspectives and make effective strategic decisions.

AoEA criteria

- Criterion 1. Demonstrating personal attributes and skills.

- Criterion 3. Acting as an enabler by providing support to drive delivery.

- Criterion 4. Enabling knowledge transfer through reference to up-to-date exemplars.

- Criterion 5. Demonstrating authority and professional credibility with clients.

Why this matters

Over the past 30 years the education system in England has been wrestling with a systematic school improvement challenge: namely, how to ensure that every child has a great education, no matter what their starting point in life or the educational setting that they attend. Fundamental to this has been the drive to ensure consistent and high standards of educational leadership across the system. The prevailing narrative has asserted that external support is only required as a response to weaknesses in performance and should be a brokered intervention. The systemic focus on 'intervention' as the prime rationale for external involvement risks implying that 'underperforming schools' need to be fixed by following external advice and that all other schools need not engage with external support at all. The focus of the AoEA is to ensure that all schools have access to high-quality and external expertise, whatever their Ofsted rating. Moreover, regular and routine external advisory work with all schools is vital so that support can be responsive at the first signs of challenging issues and not after the impact is being felt by children and young people.

I have had the privilege of working in a variety of external adviser roles, both while as a serving headteacher as a National Strategies Consultant Leader and School Improvement Partner and also as part of a large local authority school improvement workforce with very strong support from the mixed community of schools. While the context and frameworks for these roles have differed, there has been an inescapable truth: that affecting improvement as an external adviser relies on building rapport and strong relationships with school leaders.

To be clear at the outset, high-quality advisory work is dependent on being able to critically evaluate organisational effectiveness and determine what might be done in response to improvement areas. It is evidence informed, appreciative of a range of approaches and focused on impact above all else. There has to be real substance in the advice of advisers. For that advice to take seed and be influential, what I argue here is that effective advisory work requires working in concert with a leadership team, in other words working together and jointly. The adviser's focus is on enabling those working in the school to see the impact of their own decisions and provision on children and young people and then to understand what might be done differently to prompt further improvement.

In the following paragraphs I offer some pointers as to what has worked well for me personally and the teams I have led in a variety of contexts and challenges.

Establishing context and professional relationships

The contexts for the commissioning of external advisers vary greatly and each has implications for the initial engagement conversation with the leadership. A school leadership team seeking external support can have many motivations, including challenge and external perspective but also validation and preparation for an impending regulatory inspection. Schools subject to some form of external intervention, commissioned by the trust or authority that has some accountability for school performance, recognise the high stakes involved in their work with the adviser. It is very important to strike up a rapport with school leaders quickly but this cannot be at the expense of transparency. Schools should expect that the work of the adviser will be independent, evidence based and accurate, and not predetermined by the motivations of those who commission and pay for the work, whether that is the school or an external accountability partner. Advisers must quickly establish professional trust with school leaders and demonstrate that they are working authentically, with the best interests of children and young people firmly in focus.

Working in concert with a school's leadership team implies working over a period of time and not simply on a single visit. At the outset, or as early as possible, it is important to agree with leaders clear and mutual expectations of outcomes and protocols. This will involve the need to explore and agree the focus for the external adviser, within overall improvement objectives, and the required pace of any improvement journey. This is sometimes strongly influenced by the context of external influences and internal capacity.

'The focus of leadership naturally changes as a school improves. But different phases are identifiable in turning schools around and moving them on' (Matthews et al, 2014, para 94, p 36).

A helpful step might be to consider and agree with the school leadership team which of these four broad improvement contexts, developed from a research report published by the Isos Partnership, best fit.

> - Seriously underperforming or 'inadequate' school: The need is for **rescue** or recovery: rapid control, arrest of decline, assessment of priorities, firm action, critical decisions, modelling what is needed.
>
> - School that requires improvement to be judged 'good': Such a school requires **reinforcement**: building capacity, harnessing good practice and improving that which is not, developing and empowering staff, ensuring consistency, raising aspirations, designing and implementing a strategy for creating a school that is good or better.
>
> - 'Good' to 'outstanding': The task involves **refinement**: ensuring that all teaching and learning is good and that an increasingly high proportion is outstanding, refining monitoring and evaluation, ensuring that the needs of every pupil are met, growing leaders, reducing achievement gaps and maximising progress and outcomes.
>
> - Sustaining excellence: This requires attention to **renewal**: not simply sustaining outstanding practice but building on it, innovating, fine tuning and spreading the school's influence more widely.
>
> (Matthews et al, 2014, para 94, p 36)

Using expertise wisely to engage and deepen understanding

School improvement professionals with credibility and confidence will necessarily have been successful in their own school leadership. However, conversely, this can be a barrier to effective engagement in another leader's school. There is a temptation to look for what worked well for advisers in their leadership success and be sceptical of what is different or jars with personal preferences and biases. An effective adviser is capable of leaving their own professional ego at the door and recognises their own triggers for negative reactions to what they see or hear. Without this discipline, advisers can appear to school leaders as simply waiting for an opportunity to talk about themselves and what worked for them. This, far from helping, can lead to a superficial analysis of the issues facing a school and sometimes the school implementing strategies that are not fully understood in context. Moreover, an enthusiastic and knowledgeable external adviser can unwittingly begin to take on the driving role in lieu of the school's leaders. There is an important distinction between building the sustainable capacity of leaders and becoming that capacity, which can only ever be as a short-term fix, even if is sometimes enthusiastically welcomed by leaders and makes the adviser feel valued.

Understanding how a senior leadership team actually functions, its internal relationships and interfaces with other staff and governors, is critical to effective advisory practice. A useful starting point for this is to ask leaders directly to explain how leadership is in their school. An organisation's culture is often embedded in the ways things get done rather than necessarily in a mission statement and values, although these can describe the intended approach. A leadership team is not a single entity; the interactions and understandings that are shared or differ can influence their impact. Spending time to explore this with significant individuals and teams helps the adviser contextualise the school's current capacity. My experience is that the strength of leadership is often reflected in the clarity of understanding of the roles and the behaviours of leaders at all levels and those they lead. The role of the adviser is to establish the intended leadership approach and hold a mirror so that leaders can reflect on the extent to which that vision is being realised and, if not, why and how that is impacting the school. As before, however effective the adviser's own leadership vision and practice, it is important to respect the leaders' choices and focus on impact not method, however much it may differ from the adviser's own professional preferences and choices. Fundamentally, the adviser's role is to bring clarity to the minds of leaders about strategic options and the likely implications of choosing those options. It is for leaders to make those decisions and account for their impact in the future.

Advisory skills

The critical skills for an effective adviser are respect and empathy. I can honestly say that I have never worked with a school's leadership team who came into work each morning intent on holding back children's success, creating organisational confusion and demoralising staff. I have always started with the presumption that leaders want to do a great job and will be motivated to change and improve when skilful advisers engage in meaningful and professional dialogue. A genuine professional interest means asking questions that help the adviser understand the school better. Holding back from leaping in with suggestions, however well intended, is important if leadership teams are to engage and develop their own understanding.

Listening and responding skills are critical to the expert adviser. When working as a National Strategies Consultant Leader, I was introduced to skills that, once honed, stood the test of time.

Active listening means:

- attending to what has been said with concentration;
- seeking frequent opportunities to clarify your understanding;
- reflecting back to leaders what they seem to be saying;
- asking relevant questions that genuinely interest or intrigue you;
- recognising the emotional feelings that are also being expressed.

Responding means:

- suspending judgement – being tentative in your own thinking;
- drawing out the ideas and experiences of leaders;
- affirming what is being said, whenever possible, which helps you to understand the leaders' lived experience and builds confidence in your intentions to help;
- using silence, as what leaders say after an uncomfortable moment is often hugely revealing – so avoid filling the gaps in the narrative with more questions or comments;
- summarising, particularly after a lengthy narrative, can really help leaders reflect;

- paraphrasing is often helpful in drawing together the understandings that leaders and the adviser can collectively own;

- taking time to think about what you are hearing and seeing and keeping your responses short.

While conversations with leaders are essential, they should be the preface to a more active form of exploration of the work of the school. On occasion, working independently of the school's leadership team to walk the school and engage with stakeholders can be helpful, but it also tends to create an inspection mentality and focus. It's better to spend as much time as possible in the company of members of the leadership team around the school and in exploratory, collaborative activities. This quickly establishes how well the school leadership knows itself and understands how the school's performance compares to others. For example, holding discussions with pupils, staff and governors with a senior leader attending in a non-participatory role, in other words not prompting the conversations, can be a great shared learning experience for leaders. Asking them afterwards what they were able to draw from the experience can give insights that are different to when they undertake the activities themselves or get feedback from others without actually hearing it themselves. Conducting pupil progress meetings with teachers is similarly revealing when observed by senior leaders. Reversing roles so that leaders observe the adviser and the adviser observes also works well. In general, the best professional learning happens when these activities are discussed, drawing upon what was observed and the effects and impacts, rather than simple feedback. Asking '*Is this what you expected to see or hear?*' or '*Is this having the impact that you want?*' are neutral, non-confrontational question starters.

Inevitably, there will be times when resistance is encountered as the adviser begins to unlock the awareness of leaders. This takes many forms, from discrediting the evidence or expertise to overthinking or circular responses. I have always seen this as a positive sign that we may be getting closer to a breakthrough in the discourse. Rather than trying to lend more weight to the evidence and argue, it can be more helpful to try to elicit more talking by the school's leaders about their concerns and doubts. It is their journey to understanding that matters most to future improvement. If resistance is repeated, then it is time to call it out and talk about why they appear to not want to engage with the process.

Conclusion

Finally, it is my belief, overwhelmingly borne out of my experiences as a school improvement professional, that impactful working results from co-construction with school leaders. It may be easier to imagine that a more reductionist view where advisers give feedback and tell leaders what to do works best, but this is simply not my experience. Even when more expedient, the impact is rarely sustained and change is not embedded. The client-focused advisory approach requires a sophisticated skill set that has to be practised and improved over time. School leaders know when an adviser is acting in an objective, knowledgeable and authentic way, using their judgement but not being judgemental. Expert advisory work is a form of facilitating leadership despite being external to school leadership. Put simply, leaders respond best when they can feel that external advisers will challenge but are also professionally invested in the school's success and that working collectively with leaders to bring about improvement matters to them.

 Further reading

Block, P (2011) *Flawless Consulting: A Guide to Getting Your Expertise Used.* New Jersey: John Wiley and Sons Inc.

 Reference

Matthews, P, Rea, S, Hill, R and Gu, Q (2014) *Freedom to Lead: A Study of Outstanding Primary School Leadership in England.* London: Isos Partnership. Reference: DFE-RR374A. [online] Available at: https://assets.publishing.service.gov.uk/media/5a74b650e5274a3cb2866918/RR374A_-_Outstanding_primaries_final_report.pdf (accessed 3 February 2024).

9 Enabling and empowering others to affect improvement

PROFESSOR DAME ALISON PEACOCK

Key learning

- Advice is a key component of a system that inspires and develops the individual teacher within the much wider context of education as a collective endeavour supported through inclusive, ethical collaboration.

- Widespread professional learning is a cornerstone of an effective education system. Advisers have a key role in supporting the development of such a system when they provide, for example, supportive and critical analysis of self-evaluation.

AoEA criteria

- Criterion 3. Acting as an enabler by providing support to drive delivery.

- Criterion 4. Enabling knowledge transfer through reference to up-to-date exemplars.

Introduction

There has been a strong focus on systemic structure and governance across English schools since 2010, with the rapid emergence of multi-academy trusts leading to an increasingly centralised model. Less attention has been paid to the professional agency of the workforce. In fact, over the last decade there has been an increasingly powerful narrative that suggests that evidence now exists that means teachers simply need to follow the script in all matters (OECD, 2016). My contention is that simply following a script, whether that is during lessons or following a flow chart of actions regarding behaviour management, risks education becoming a workforce of technicians as opposed to a professional learning community. It is my belief that we need a knowledgeable, informed, agentic profession that nevertheless benefits from ideas and practices that support working practice at scale. In this chapter I argue for a profession inspired by the importance of phronesis, professional intuitive wisdom informed by relevant and important research, supported and enabled by a compassionate tier of educational advisers who act as enablers for the system and enable knowledge transfer.

Enabling change

There is a central urgency at the heart of education, which is to strive to make things better – to utilise the scant resources that we have to ensure that children and young people have the very best schooling possible. For me, providing the 'very best' means offering a rich, broad curriculum, both academic and vocational, to all. It means commitment to every child to make schooling the beginning of education for life, for future careers but also to engage meaningfully in community and society at large, aiming for a collective sense of what it means to be human. It means helping each teacher to flourish, to achieve success and to welcome skilful mentoring.

I am proud to consider myself to be a teacher, first and foremost. I have worked in a wide variety of schools across early years, primary and secondary and have also spent time supporting the learning of children with moderate learning difficulties. Throughout my career, which has been characterised by a restless ambition to constantly improve, I have sought to deepen an understanding of how research and the wider improvement agenda can be made to benefit children. In relatively recent years there has been a relentless focus on target setting, applying business management theory to education. This in part led to the nonsensical approach of micro-measurement and comparison of individual class cohorts via flawed tracking systems from which management teams were encouraged to draw (often) completely erroneous conclusions. I am proud to have been part of the movement that called for a change of emphasis, a move away from tracking to informed assessment. Scrapping national curriculum levels was an important part of shifting the improvement narrative away from individual teacher performance towards whole school development. Additionally, the decision of the inspectorate to refuse to engage with internal tracking data meant that supposed 'evidence' of school improvement needed to be sought elsewhere.

Building teacher professionalism and leadership

In 2016, the government provided initial grant funding for the establishment of the Chartered College of Teaching (CCoT). Five million pounds was allocated over a period of four years, coming to an end in March 2020 just as the Covid-19 pandemic struck. Fortunately, membership income, research and project income plus philanthropic support has meant that the College has been able to transition beyond government funding to becoming a completely independent, non-partisan charity. The mission of the College is to '*empower a trusted, knowledgeable profession through membership and accreditation*' (Chartered College of Teaching, 2023). Through voluntary individual or group membership, our mission is to celebrate the growth and intellectual development of teachers and those working alongside them to continually learn, develop and share. Tens of thousands of teachers have joined the College and we have also started to attract the interest of those working in British international schools across 82 countries. Collaboration at scale is inspired by the collective view that what unites the profession is far greater than anything that divides us. The publication of a themed peer-reviewed journal provides an opportunity for teachers and academics to write alongside one another in an embodiment of the vision for phronesis. There is a constant balancing act to ensuring that our journal content, our online events, our commentary is led by the opinions and response from our members and that the College maintains a safe space for professional debate. Essentially, we seek to transcend the politics of the day, engaging the profession in respectful dialogue.

The implementation of widespread professional learning via the National Professional Qualifications is to be welcomed, but alongside helping colleagues to scale the 'golden thread' of career development the College is also very keen that we help classroom teachers to further review and develop their practice within the classroom.

The demise of the Advanced Skills teacher pay grade at the beginning of the last decade meant that many teachers seeking promotion looked to leadership routes rather than being rewarded for staying in the classroom. We have developed rigorous Chartered accreditation routes, which include online assessments and exams, providing strong recognition for teachers wishing to enhance and develop their pedagogical practice. Testimony from those who have completed the programme speaks of the 'boundless potential' of professional learning to impact classroom practice.

In 2019, the work of a commission of representatives from professional organisations published the Ethical Leadership Framework (Roberts, 2019). The Chartered College agreed to place this work at the heart of the College, and from January 2024 all prospective Fellows of the College will be asked to agree to abide by the Nolan principles of public life alongside the virtues of ethical leadership:

- selflessness;
- integrity;
- objectivity;
- accountability;
- openness;
- honesty;
- leadership.

The Ethical Leadership Framework (Roberts, 2019) emphasises the importance of leading with the following personal characteristics or virtues:

- trust;
- wisdom;
- kindness;
- justice;
- service;
- courage;
- optimism.

The hope is that the framework with associated virtues will act as a reminder for all those in leadership positions of the huge responsibility they bear not only to their peers but to wider society (Roberts, 2019). In a chapter about enabling and effecting school improvement it is important that we reflect on the kind of culture we wish to build, support and nurture. Within this context the Chartered College is leading a national conversation about the nature of professionalism. We believe a collective recognition and appreciation of what professionalism encompasses helps all of us to feel united in our strength of purpose and commitment. It is important for the morale and well-being of our teachers and school leaders that the standing of our profession is held in high regard within our communities. As the College of Teaching we are committed to seeking, celebrating and sharing the very best practice. So what does it mean to be a professional? Sachs (2003) differentiates between old and new professionalism (see Table 9.1).

Table 9.1 Characteristics of old and new professionalism

Old professionalism	New professionalism
Exclusive membership	Inclusive membership
Conservative practices	Public ethical code of practice
Self-interest	Collaborative and collegial
External regulation	Activist orientation
Slow to change	Flexible
Reactive	Responsive
	Self-regulating
	Policy active
	Enquiry oriented
	Knowledge building

'New' professionalism assigns an active role to teachers as knowledge builders and producers, thus emphasising the role of the teacher alongside the collaborative in developing and refining practice.

We have reviewed the literature and put forward the following aspects of professionalism for discussion:

- a strong knowledge base that combines research evidence and teacher expertise;
- research literacy that allows teachers to read, critique and implement research findings and conduct their own research to further advance knowledge in the sector;
- a high level of autonomy that allows teachers to take the decisions that are right for their context and students;
- strong peer networks that allow teachers to exchange with and learn from others;
- high-quality professional development opportunities;
- professional standards that are developed and owned by the profession and drive professional excellence;
- a profession that is driven by high ethical standards, acting in the interest of their students and society more widely;
- a focus on teacher well-being, so teachers have the time and energy to engage in professional learning and deliver high-quality teaching;
- teachers' active involvement in policy decisions that affect them.

Advising for improvement

Thus far, I have discussed the role of the school-based professional as a means for improvement. There is also a very powerfully influential role for the external adviser in helping individual schools and groups of schools to self-evaluate. The initial multi-academy trust (MAT) building phase which has characterised the last decade must now give space to look beyond internal expertise towards considering regional differences and characteristics. Groups of schools working together, as happened during the pandemic, is often helpfully facilitated by colleagues who have the privilege of working beyond one particular group. The benefits of wise counsel from an objective adviser can be transformative. I am a great supporter of the Association of Education Advisers (AoEA), established at a similar time as the College to offer accreditation to individual consultants advising schools. A system that is supported in this manner has a greater chance of continuous outward-facing development, supporting those within the MAT or local authority but with the benefit of objective external assessment.

School improvement starts with support for the individual teacher, their department or phase and ultimately encompassing the whole school within a community as the engine for inspiration and knowledge building.

As I write, interesting collaboratives of schools and MATs are beginning work to address some of the wide-ranging systemic issues that massively impact on the work of those in education. In Greater Manchester there is interest in providing an alternative to the EBacc via a broader suite of subjects for study and collective assessment 14–18 years. In Teesside a collective of MATs, the university and others are coming together to debate what can be done to alleviate some of the worst impact of family poverty. In the south-west a large group of school leaders convened by a MAT leader, with informal support from the Regional Director, meet regularly to debate how attainment can be positively impacted through greater collaboration.

It seems clear that regional leadership and resource provision of education must become a priority of a future government, but in the meantime school leaders and consultants are tackling the job in hand with increasing confidence and innovation. Advisers from the AoEA working with the Chartered College membership, together with other like-minded organisations, stands a good chance of building a system that inspires and develops the individual teacher within the much wider context of education as a collective endeavour supported through inclusive, ethical collaboration.

References

Chartered College of Teaching (2023). [online] Available at: https://chartered.college (accessed 8 February 2024).

Organisation for Economic Co-operation and Development (OECD) (2016) *Supporting Teacher Professionalism: Insights from TALIS 2013*. Paris: OECD Publishing. https://doi.org/10.1787/9789264248601-en

Roberts, C (2019) *Ethical Leadership for a Better Education System*. Abingdon: Routledge.

Sachs, J (2003) *The Activist Teaching Profession*. Buckingham: Open University Press.

10 Building an advisory community in Northern Ireland

MARY LOWERY

Key learning

- Understanding context is the basis of a programme of change.

- Unity of purpose and shared values fortify a community.

- Expectations and modelling cultivate professional language and behaviour.

AoEA criteria

- Criterion 1. Demonstrating personal attributes and skills.

- Criterion 4. Enabling knowledge transfer through reference to up-to-date exemplars.

- Criterion 5. Demonstrating authority and professional credibility with clients.

Introduction

This chapter explores how, within the framework of the Association of Education Advisers' (AoEA) accreditation programme, the Education Authority in Northern Ireland is growing a system-wide, high-quality advisory community, engaging colleagues, educational partners and school leaders.

Context

On 1 April 2015, the educational administration in Northern Ireland was transformed from five Education and Library Boards to one single regional structure: the Education Authority (EA). The Authority comprises five Directorates, of which Education is one.

Within the Education Directorate, an extensive Curriculum Advisory and Support Service (CASS) of over two hundred officers was dissolved and a School Development Service (SDS) of around 30 staff created. The service comprised both former CASS colleagues and newly appointed personnel. The remit of officers changed from a mainly curricular focus, with a subject specialism, to a more strategic support and challenge function.

The change was largely regarded by schools, and by a proportion of the workforce, as a deficit rather than a transformation. It was referred to in those terms. This perception, coupled with interruptions in service due to the protracted restructuring and recruitment process, impacted the credibility of and system confidence in the new EA.

Concurrent with the establishment of the EA, a number of educational partner organisations were becoming increasingly engaged in school improvement work. All were united in intent, but there was a need to reach commonality in understanding, language and practice, in order to provide cohesive, high-quality support and challenge for school improvement at system level across Northern Ireland.

With this in mind, EA connected with the AoEA, an independent, professional association providing a focused accreditation and development programme for school advisers. Their core belief in human potential, that every child wants to learn, and every teacher wants to teach, accorded strongly with our own. A new professional community was born.

Intention

At a delivery level, the core objective in working in partnership with AoEA was to develop a high-quality school improvement service to schools by:

- engaging SDS and educational partners in professional development and accreditation relevant to their roles;

- improving cross-organisational and cross-jurisdiction connections;

- providing access to a current, high-quality professional network and knowledge base to maintain the quality of the service;

- raising and sustaining the credibility of the service with stakeholders through the accreditation and through the outworking of the new learning in schools.

At a strategic level, through the partnership we aimed to:

- support the development of a consistent language, understanding and practice around school improvement across our service and our partners;

- provide a forum where colleagues could learn together and alongside partners, in a professional community engaged in similar work;

- build and sustain a culture of good self-directed professional learning habits;

- challenge our thinking through exposure to educational perspectives from beyond our jurisdiction;

- challenge and review our understanding of what professional development looks like and so influence our work with schools in this regard;

- learn from the modelling of high-quality professional development and facilitation to support improvement in these in our service.

The programme aimed to enrich thinking and practice, and to influence across, upwards and outwards into the education system, for the development of everyone involved.

Year 1: school improvement professionals

Following an initial briefing from AoEA and on an open invitation, we engaged a pilot cohort of 18 colleagues and peers across partner organisations in the AoEA Associate accreditation process.

Aside from successful accreditation, the emerging impact was very significant. On evaluation of the experience, participants were unanimous in their endorsement of the approaches taken: the tone, the relevance and quality of the provision, the opportunities to discuss with colleagues from within and beyond Northern Ireland and the changes in their thinking and practice as a result. Key developmental points noted in participants' evaluations included:

- an improving clarity as to our role and the associated attributes, skills and knowledge, through self- and peer assessment against the criteria;

- increasingly courageous and honest self-evaluation, supported by the professional discussion in the accreditation process;

- sharper, more disciplined critical reflection on our own work, through writing the portfolio;

- improved quality of discussion and improved cross-organisational relationships following participation in the breakout rooms during the courses;

- improved leadership development work with schools in, for example, coaching, curriculum planning and change management.

The detailed evaluative comments from initial participants is itself evidence of the power of the experience and the value placed on it by those who engaged. Bottom-up and inside-out change was happening: we were beginning to realise the intentions of the programme.

Conversations with and among accredited Associates, their visible application of the learning and a tangible sense of achievement and professional pride generated curiosity across the service and partners, as well as increased demand for a second cohort.

Year 2: school improvement professionals and school leaders

Second and third cohorts of EA colleagues and partners followed, totalling a further 40 participants.

A selection process was devised, requiring one case study of a targeted intervention, which could then be used in the AoEA accreditation process. This afforded EA leadership a better understanding of the accreditation programme and an overview of the diversity and quality of the work of officers while confirming participants' commitment to the process from the outset.

The learning and impact of the programme were already in evidence in teams beyond SDS, so it was made available to other services across the Education Directorate, including School Governance, Community and Schools, and our educational technology team.

Potential to extend the offer to school leaders had always been under consideration: such an approach could strengthen the outworking of the programme across the system and support succession planning for future advisory services. Furthermore, it would contribute to the implementation of 'Learning Leaders' (Department of Education NI, 2016), the Department of Education Strategy for Teacher Professional Learning.

The timing of a funding allocation for the professional development and well-being of school leaders, through the *A Fair Start* report (Department of Education NI, 2021), made this a possibility. School leaders, however, were exhausted from the intensity and high alert required during Covid-19 management. Many were deflated from having navigated a context of teacher industrial action since January 2017, which had curtailed initiatives for improvement and approaches to quality assurance in the system, most notably school inspections.

That said, we experience daily the strong sense of moral purpose and service that drives so many of our school leaders. The motivation to constantly improve what they provide for the children and young people thrives, completely independent of external or other quality assurance imperatives. School leaders continue to seek high-quality, challenging professional development. In Northern Ireland, we have had no Professional Qualification for Headship (PQHNI) for several years and, at the time of writing, there is no other accredited development programme for experienced school leaders outside of self-funded university courses.

Challenges remained, though: we were offering a new way of learning, facilitated by a new partner from outside our jurisdiction, to a traditionally careful and exacting group of professionals, in a most challenging educational context. Together with AoEA, and speaking from our own experience, we introduced our school leaders to the people and the programme.

Year 3: strangers, visitors ... early advocates

Given the challenging context, we invited an open expression of interest, which attracted over 80 school leaders.

We are a small jurisdiction: credibility, trust and strong interpersonal relationships are key to how we function. Managing the cohort of school leaders was characterised by intermittent individual communication, phone calls and online conversations, where candidates shared their experiences at all stages, encouraged each other and advised as to what would be helpful for future cohorts.

At the end of the school year, we held a most uplifting celebration event for the school leaders and colleagues, supported by all partners involved and the Department of Education.

EA colleagues, partners and a number of principals attended the AoEA Annual Summit in York in July during our school holidays, a strong statement, especially in the industrial relations climate.

As with the EA colleagues and partners, the impact of the programme on the professional development, mindset and motivation of school leaders was marked. One principal stated that the programme had repurposed her so powerfully it had been the deciding factor in her change of heart around early retirement. Consistently, principals communicated appreciation of the following:

- professional affirmation and recognition of their competence;
- high-quality professional dialogue in the accreditation process;
- excellent quality and immediate relevance of the course content to their work;
- opportunities to think strategically again post-Covid-19;

- opportunities to connect with colleagues in other educational phases and organisations;

- the appropriateness of format, quality and range of presenters at the fortnightly EduKITs;

- access to the books authored by facilitators and their rejuvenated interest in professional reading;

- the sense of achievement from documenting their own school improvement work and from attaining accreditation.

All of this in a climate of significant industrial action and in a post-pandemic landscape.

Year 4: our advisory community

As we enter the fourth year of partnership working with AoEA, we continue to build our advisory community across and beyond Northern Ireland.

We have realised our initial objectives in:

- engaging SDS and educational partners in professional development and accreditation relevant to their roles;

- improving cross-organisational and cross-jurisdiction connections;

- providing access to a current, relevant, high-quality professional network and knowledge base to maintain the quality of the service.

We have gone much further: 200 colleagues from the EA, educational partners and schools have engaged in the programme. One-tenth of our school leaders have been learning and developing alongside advisory colleagues from educational partners, opening conversations, building relationships, collegiality and trust across the system, raising the level of professional dialogue and bringing a degree of coherence to how we approach school development.

Through the online facilitation, doors have been opened to professional learning and sharing across jurisdictions: connections have been made at organisational and at individual level. Northern Irish colleagues are increasingly visible and taking the lead at cross-jurisdiction AoEA events. Different voices are being heard. While growing and enhancing our own advisory community in Northern Ireland, we have become part of a larger professional community whose future we are helping to shape.

Lessons from the partnership

In sharing lessons learned from the work outlined, it is important to state the following.

- Start with a small cohort.
- Plan the process tightly.
- Communicate the overall time and expectations.
- Keep the processes and communication tight – stay in touch with participants and keep them in touch with each other.
- Maintain a balance between autonomy and accountability.
- Keep faith that people will want to engage and compete – the quality of the offer is motivation in itself.
- Capture participants' evaluations throughout.
- Keep sustainability and legacy in mind from the beginning.

For us, the most significant factor in building our advisory community within this partnership has underpinned every interaction from the beginning. It is not new, and it is not complex, though it is not always named. It is that values, and how people live them out in language and behaviour, are at the heart of every authentic change.

The values of the AoEA are lived out in their respect for learners, teachers and for us as an educational community. Their values chime with ours and this has been, and remains, the strength of the partnership. For that, there is no substitute.

Further reading

Hargreaves, A and O'Connor, M T (2018) *Collaborative Professionalism.* Thousand Oaks, CA: Corwin.

References

Department of Education NI (2016) *Learning Leaders: A Strategy for Teacher Professional Learning.* [online] Available at: https://ccea.org. uk/learning-leaders (accessed 3 February 2024).

Department of Education NI (2021) *Expert Panel on Educational Underachievement in Northern Ireland. A Fair Start: Final Report & Action Plan, May 2021.* [online] Available at: www.education-ni.gov.uk/publications/fair-start-final-report-action-plan (accessed 3 February 2024).

11 How to be an international education adviser

PROFESSOR ANDY HARGREAVES

Key learning

- Understanding and responding to complexity are ever-present aspects of the advisory role: when they are embraced, then thoughtful, creative approaches emerge.

- Be both confident and pro-active in your approach: have the courage to develop your own methods and approaches and use them skilfully and adaptively to create change.

- Harness the power of collaboration, creating teams with varied expertise who can consider the many dimensions of a situation.

AoEA criteria

- Criterion 1. Demonstrating personal attributes and skills.

- Criterion 2. Ability to challenge and work within agreed protocols.

- Criterion 3. Acting as an enabler by providing support to drive delivery.

- Criterion 5. Demonstrating authority and professional credibility with clients.

Forty years ago, when I was too young to advise anyone about anything, a senior colleague was appointed to lead a major review of a large system. '*What impact do you think your recommendations will have?*', I asked him. '*Well*', he replied, '*it's in the nature of advice that you can ignore it!*'

This insight is both humbling and liberating. It's humbling because advisers have no inherent power or mandate to implement or impose anything. It's liberating because that very fact also means that, given their temporary status and having none of the worries about job security that permanent employees have, international advisers have the freedom to suggest things that no one else can.

I've been offering policy advice of one sort or another for 30 years with varying degrees of success. Some of this arises out of other functions such as reporting to policymakers on research and on recommendations arising from it. Some of it is more formal – an appointment to undertake a policy review, perhaps – or it might be a semi-permanent position with the title of adviser officially attached to it. The role can be with a particular government or with transnational organisations in education. It may involve a single meeting or it might extend to a long-term contract. Advisory work in all these situations comes with little accountability, but it can carry immense responsibility.

'*How did you become an adviser?*' I'm sometimes asked. The answer is that you don't really plan to become an adviser. Rather, over many years, if you do good work, if you intend as part of it to get its results into the public domain, if you learn to communicate clearly and accessibly in person and in print, and if you do work that is relevant to people in policy, then eventually, at some point, when your values are synchronised, policymakers will approach you, not vice versa.

I've often referenced my status as an adviser, and I have publicly shared some of the results of my advisory work. This is the first time I have had an opportunity to reflect on the nature of the work itself and to consider how best to approach it. This brief chapter unpacks some of those reflections in the form of ten pieces of advice for other would-be advisers, supported by examples and, in some cases, confessions from my own experiences.

1. Convergent goals

Be clear about how your own goals fit with those of the people hiring you. Don't be flattered into joining something you don't believe in. You may have to live with a few things that you don't normally support, but if your main directions are aligned then you will have a good match. The job of an adviser is largely to help a system achieve those goals. There are exceptions though. When I began working with one system I advised, its minister's chief goal was to score higher on the international PISA tests than the neighbouring country within less than two years. This was manifestly absurd, and my fellow reviewers and I told them. But it was also clear that other people in the policy system hungered for something deeper than this, and, taking advantage of a change in minister, we successfully advised them to reconnect their educational ambitions with what they wanted to recapture and reinvent for themselves educationally and culturally as a system and as a nation. Instead of racking up a higher competitive score, we helped them rediscover their identity.

2. Owning, not renting

I have seen high-priced consulting teams go from country to country advising on improvement and reform, with almost the same PowerPoint deck. Only the opening slide changes. There is also a temptation for people who have held senior positions in a system that has achieved global recognition for high performance to oversell that country's methods and accomplishments to others. The systems vary – England, Ontario, Finland, Singapore, Shanghai and, most recently, Estonia, for example. Every country, culture or system is unique in some ways though – so borrowing or renting pre-packaged solutions from single exemplars elsewhere is likely to bring eventual disappointment. It's best for a system to find and own its own solution, drawing on evidence and examples from many places, not just one. The job of an adviser with integrity is to connect systems with a range of evidence and examples that will help them learn and improve in their own way – not to impose pre-packaged solutions and templates to which they have become attached but that turn out to be culturally and politically insensitive.

3. Yes and no, Minister

You may have been hired by a government or an international organisation, but ultimately your job is to improve things for young people and their teachers. To do this, you will need to be able to read the internal politics of the system. Many executives and bureaucracies try to 'run' their minister. If it is the minister who wants you as an adviser, the executive will try to run you too – giving you only the information they think you need and deluging you with PowerPoint presentations. Or they will try to ensure you don't get a chance to meet alone with the minister without them. Conversely, if the executive hires you, sometimes they will use your expertise to change the minister's mind or to go around them. You must figure this out and then act. In my first ever advisory role, the Deputy Minister (Executive) deliberately released our report and recommendations to every school in the province without seeking the minister's permission, and then apologised once he really had let the cat out of the bag. Another minister I met with then announced a major change in the nation's testing system without warning the civil servants, knowing that they would oppose it – which made them wonder where on earth the idea had come from!

4. Key moments

When you're playing a team sport, much of the game is spent holding your shape and jockeying for position. But every so often, there will be a key moment, an opening in the play or a mistake by one's opponents. Seizing that may determine the difference between victory and defeat. Playing the role of adviser is no different. Watch out for key moments and take them when they come. In a senior-level meeting with one system's top political leader and all the education ministry executive, the members of our advisory team were asked in turn to make observations on how the government was faring in implementing its policies. I had data, critical data, relating to one of the government's policies. I sensed a chance to bring about a change. Each adviser offered an observation. The most senior expert in the room went first. I waited until last. It was hard and risky. We could have run out of time when it came round to my turn. But the last word is usually the one that sticks. I made favourable reference to the government's and leader's priority on improving child well-being. But the policy I had evidence on, I said, was harming children and creating ill-being. I was sure, I added, that the leader did not want this. So, I asked, indeed begged, the leader to change the policy for the sake of children's well-being. The executive rushed off into a frenzy of attempted damage limitation. But the leader was moved to commission a review, which recommended reversing many aspects of the policy and which the leader officially accepted.

5. Yesterday's news

Every so often, advice you've offered or a review you've undertaken may cause a controversy. It may make news headlines and you may feel inclined to rush in and react. But as one minister said to his advisory team, today's news headlines are tomorrow's chip papers (the ones your fish and chips get wrapped in!). Some years ago, when I was working in Ontario, we were doing a government-funded study of secondary school change. In the middle of all this, a newly elected government took office and implemented a set of policies that had disastrous consequences for schools. Our ongoing study was able to pick all this up. Our final report was very critical of the new government, so I sent a draft to a trusted member of the ministry bureaucracy, asking if any alterations would increase its chance of acceptance. He advised me that when you write a report you need to decide whether you are inside the system, trying to tweak it, or outside, trying to fight it. And, he went on, it was very clear where our report stood on that question and so we probably didn't want to change it. We then did a surprise press release on it on a day I was overseas. The government immediately called the dean of our faculty. They demanded that he instantly walk over to Parliament with a physical copy of the report. They also threatened to withdraw all research funding from the faculty. Faculty administration was frantic. But the dean assured them that it would be a forgotten part of the news cycle in a couple of days and that I'd sort things out when I got back. It was. And I did. Just tomorrow's chip papers! Nothing more.

6. Backstage

When you're a senior adviser, there's never a backstage. Treat nothing like it's off the record. Never over-share. You probably see yourself as an academic or an educational leader who happens to be a government adviser. But others – the media, government opponents and rival countries – will regard you as being a key adviser, close to the seats of power, who just happens to be an academic or another kind of educator. To them, you're worth investing in. Be careful what you put in your emails because at some point, Freedom of Information requests may come. If you're in a country that is not a democracy, watch out for espionage. I've arrived by surprise back in my luxury hotel room to find 'servants' hurriedly putting away my bags that they had probably been searching through. I was interrogated for two hours leaving one country about every hour I had spent there, probably because of one sentence raising questions about its government's policy in my presentation. In some countries, devices or mirrors in your room may be wired for surveillance. So, think twice about what you do there. Should adoring graduate students or translators head with you back towards your hotel room, do not take up any hints or accept any offers. If you're normally a 6 out of 10 in these stakes in your own country and you get treated as a 9 overseas, there's a reason for that, and it's not a good one. Don't drink too much. It can lead you to drop your guard. Beware of lucrative offers, like the multi-million-dollar contract I was offered to evaluate a nation's law-enforcement training system. It may be used to compromise or neutralise you ethically later. When travelling to certain countries, you may best be advised to leave your laptop, tablet and even your phone at home, and to purchase a temporary phone instead. Overall, the humblest position you can adopt is not to believe you're nobody, but to accept that, in other people's eyes, you are a potentially significant somebody. Last, but by no means least, different cultures will have rules regarding what you cannot talk about. What do you do? If you choose to go, you respect the culture.

7. On message

One of the first questions I often get asked when having a one-time meeting with a minister is what are three things that I would advise them to do in their country? Not five, seven or ten. But three. Ministers, the media and senior policy officials don't want long lists, rambling stories, a profusion of examples and being told how complicated things are. They want expert, informed, advice with actionable directions. Similarly, while whimsical, mercurial, quixotic comments might be stimulating and entertaining in an academic seminar, they don't usually sit well around a cabinet table. Stay on topic. Don't go off-piste. Don't take the bait of questions like the one from a Spanish newspaper seeking a comment related to Catalan independence movements when its reporter asked me: '*You work for the separatist Nicola Sturgeon (of Scotland)! What are your opinions about nationalism?*' (I replied that our educational advisory work was not concerned with nationalism and that our meetings never discussed it.) Stick with your areas of expertise. Stay calm. Avoid getting irritated by questions like the one I was asked by a radio station about low teachers' pay: '*So, does this mean if you pay peanuts, you get monkeys?*' If you're going into a high-stress, high-stakes situation like a parliamentary committee or a national media interview, prepare very thoroughly beforehand, and then, confident in what you know, relax and be authoritative but approachable on the occasion itself. And don't be shy about having a few sound bites in your back pocket. One national leader said that one thing they liked about working with me was that I gave them valuable turns of phrase to support their policies during parliamentary question time.

8. Nothing lasts forever

In politics, it is sometimes said, there are no permanent friends or permanent enemies. Governments lose elections. Ministers and other senior officials turn over. Agendas shift. Scandals happen. Money runs out. Close advisory relationships can come to an end in an instant. Nothing lasts forever in politics, business or funding agencies. So, when there is an affinity between your goals and those of a system and its leaders, treat it as a window that is open but that will not always stay open. This is when you can become a critical friend for a system or a global organisation. In time, though, the window will shut when leaders and agendas change and are no longer in alignment with your own values or, in your view, with the needs of young people and their teachers. Then you must consider opposing those in power and becoming a public intellectual who uses their expertise to mobilise opposition to a system's bad direction or wrongdoing. The main thing to grasp is that when the window is open, behave like it is open. And when it is closed, behave like it is closed. Don't get good at a bad game with a bad system, as my colleague and friend Michael

Fullan has argued. But don't continue to be contrarian for its own sake when a good system is headed in a positive direction either.

9. Teams

Multiple advisers working in teams are better than single advisers going it alone. The adviser's enemy here is their own ego and narcissism. Some years ago, I was approached to be the education adviser for a political leader. I declined the offer. Single advisers of high-profile leaders can come to be seen as a Svengali figure that's pulling all the strings behind the scenes. This undermines the authority of the leader. Or they come to be regarded as a puppet of the system who is there to legitimise its actions. This undermines the reputation of the adviser. Instead, I successfully proposed a team of advisers on the grounds that the leader needs to make final decisions based on a diversity of advice – not so much from individuals but from a team striving to help establish a direction from this diversity. One of the most highly regarded activities of the OECD (Organisation for Economic Co-operation and Development) according to the education ministers of its member countries is the reviews it conducts for the policies of specific countries, at their request. After discussion with the systems in question, the OECD compiles teams of about four members, including two outside experts, to review data and documents and then visits the system for an intensive week of observations and interviews with multiple stakeholders. I have been on four of these teams where we work together practically every minute of the day, reviewing our perceptions and working theories over breakfasts and dinners, tapping away on our laptops, as our understandings and then recommendations begin to unfold. We come with different expertise, we are open to each other's perceptions, and we work collaboratively for a common, helpful and practical outcome that is presented to the system.

10. Enjoy

In the middle of all the work, controversy and complexity, don't neglect to enjoy your role. You have spent years building up expertise on which your advice will be based. You likely came into education to make a difference, and now there's a chance that you can – big time! Don't pass up the opportunity. Be bold but not brusque. Speak your mind but out of the need to influence, not the drive to perform. More than any permanent employee, you may be the one everyone is looking to for offering something different, ideas out of the box, and solutions that challenge conventional wisdom and vested interests. Of course, some may regard your advice as *too* bold. But remember – it is in the nature of advice that they can ignore it. And the worst they can do is fire you. In the end, always remember your North Star. Being a high-level international adviser should not be about power, ego, self-indulgence, photo-ops with your political heroes or staying relevant in old age. It should be about the millions of young people whose lives you have a glorious opportunity to help improve.

A culminating example

At some point, if you have developed diverse experiences of international advising, it's worth considering creating something that can take advice to systems rather than systems always coming to you. Starting in 2016, in collaboration with my Norwegian colleague Yngve Lindvig, I created an international network we named the ARC Education Collaboratory. This network, or perhaps it is even a movement, began as a counter to established transnational organisations and to national policy systems that were still preoccupied with testing and technology. It was a response to many system leaders confiding in me and in some of my colleagues that there had to be better policy directions than this.

ARC was established in a meeting in a restaurant on a cold night in Toronto. It is a group of countries serving democracies and it is about democracies that promote human rights. Before Covid-19, it met at an annual summit to engage with local schools and be stimulated by internationally regarded thought leaders who also donated their time for free, and it worked in facilitated groups of trusted peers who coached each other on significant problems of policy together. During Covid-19, ARC's work continued virtually every two months and addressed compelling issues that systems were dealing with during the pandemic such as well-being, learning outdoors and high school examinations. As a result of being in ARC, some systems have changed their policies on well-being, provided outdoor learning spaces for every elementary school, rethought high school examinations and upgraded the priority they give to vocational education.

Last word

Life is not a rehearsal. If you value having your work, ideas and expertise entering the public domain and you want to work with systems that share them and to publicly oppose systems that do not, by working with an opposition party or a teachers' union, perhaps, do not pass up the opportunity when it comes to you. You will not regret it. You will not always succeed. But as the iconic Canadian hockey star Wayne Gretsky has put it, '*You miss 100% of the shots you don't take*'.

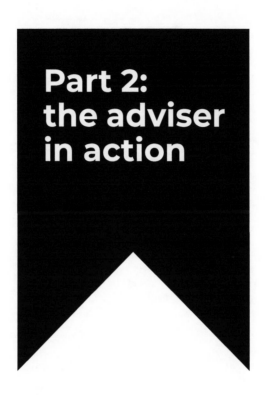

Part 2: the adviser in action

12 Building social capital: learning to 'THRiVE'

FRAZER BAILIE

Key learning

- The chapter outlines characteristics of genuine community partnership.

- Certain conditions are required to create an impactful 'multiplier effect' across communities.

- Clarity and strength are necessary for collaborative leadership.

AoEA criteria

- Criterion 1. Demonstrating personal attributes and skills.

- Criterion 3. Acting as an enabler by providing support to drive delivery.

- Criterion 5. Demonstrating authority and professional credibility with clients

Introduction

This chapter describes how THRiVE, a collaboration of community members, voluntary groups, charities, schools, government agencies and a local council, partnered to maximise learners' achievements in a Neighbourhood Renewal Area (Noble Multiple Deprivation Measure [placing this ward in the most deprived 10 per cent of wards across Northern Ireland]).

Context

This Protestant working-class community is situated near the shores of Belfast Lough, and it is deemed to be a pocket of significant economic and social need.

Despite the success of the 1998 Good Friday Agreement (The Belfast Agreement, 1998), this community has been prioritised for support via the Northern Ireland Assembly's Tackling Paramilitarism, Criminality and Organised Crime Programme. This programme aims to '*Break the cycle of paramilitary activity and organised crime, and to stop another generation getting drawn into the spiral*' (Northern Island Assembly, 2015).

The impact of paramilitarism is compounded by low incomes, multi-generational unemployment and a sense of being left behind from the prosperity created by peace.

Many studies over the years have noted the vulnerability of the Protestant working class, boys especially, and the need to support these communities more inclusively. The most current is the *A Fair Start – Final Report & Action Plan* (Department of Education NI, 2021), where a panel of experts considered this case study and others and agreed a collective approach to increase attainment.

School-led initiatives alone would not turn this tide. There was a need to try something different. The local high school provided their library for our meeting. There was a 'buzz' of expectation as parents, community and voluntary sector leaders, headteachers, education authority representatives, and health and social care administrators gathered. The challenge was to collaborate to break down the barriers that impeded their children and young people's success.

Challenge

The development of this diverse collaboration involved building social capital to bring about impactful change. It was both aspirational and transformational.

In 2012, I was appointed as headteacher of a local primary school. The school was aspirational; it was rated as outstanding and was oversubscribed. By 2015, standards in the school had improved year on year. However, we knew we needed to shift the paradigm. We needed to work differently, not harder.

I had completed a Master's degree in educational leadership in 2000. My thesis was based on building social capital to bring about impactful innovation.

I took up the challenge to work with our community partners to overcome learners' barriers to success. My vision was to evolve from my role in individual school development to actively collaborate in community improvement.

In Michael Fullan's *The Principal* (2014), he highlighted the importance of '*social capital*' to drive pedagogical innovation. I planned to build social capital beyond the school gates. I was determined to change the narrative.

Barriers to learning stemmed from economic, social and health circumstances as well as educational need. Logically the solution would be multifaceted. We needed to form an alliance of parents, community, health, social care, religious and school leaders.

The ambition was to create a partnership to work 'upstream'. The aim was to address the causes of underachievement and not just the symptoms. Put simply, the desire was for these children and young people to thrive.

Catalyst

In their book *The Intelligent School* (2004), MacGilchrist et al describe how effective schools build social capital. Influenced by their research, I created a model to visualise the relationship between collaboration and effective change (Figure 12.1).

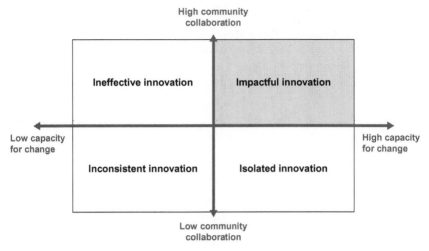

Figure 12.1 Social capital building quadrants

Quadrant 1: ineffective innovation

While these schools can engage with their communities effectively, they can lack the capacity due to factors such as leadership and/or resourcing to capitalise on their connection. They tend to underdeliver, disappoint their stakeholders and this causes 'waning social capital'.

Quadrant 2: inconsistent innovation

While these schools can innovate, they often lack the internal capacity to implement initiatives effectively. In addition, the innovations planned may not always properly align with their community's needs. These schools tend to have 'weak social capital'.

Quadrant 3: isolated innovation

While these schools innovate systematically, they may fail to match their communities' needs and/or draw upon the additionality that would enhance their work. These schools have 'wasted social capital'.

But how could we achieve this 'impactful innovation' in a community that had expressed its own frustration at its inability to collaborate effectively?

My Master's research in 2000 was shaped by an example of collaborative working conducted in a rural area in India (Singh, 1981). The local authorities wanted to promote adult education but all efforts to provide adult classes had been rejected by the community.

Singh engaged the community and asked them what they felt they needed. They prioritised building a road over adult education. Paradoxically, as they engaged in planning to build the road, they realised their need for adult education.

Reason (1994, p 3) advocates for the potential of such empowered collaborations: '*New possibilities are dreamed and brought into reality, so for a moment the world is realigned towards a new form of participant reality*'.

Collaboration

A powerful collaboration was formed. It brought together participants from education, health, social services, justice and members of the community in a 'melting pot'. It was not about handing out 'one-size-fits-all' solutions but about listening, trusting the local wisdom and facilitating change.

The collaboration was named THRiVE. Like a well-known brand of paint, 'it does what it says on the tin'. After significant engagement, the collaboration's participants came up with four key priorities that would shape THRiVE's direction. THRiVE would seek to increase community:

- aspirations;
- achievement;
- well-being;
- collaboration.

There was no resistance from community participants as they had identified the priorities. A project board was formed, including representatives from the community, voluntary and statutory bodies. This board commissioned several sub-groups who were each tasked to deliver THRiVE's four priorities to their assigned stakeholders. For example, the Schools' Sub-Group supported work to increase learners' attainment in schools and the Parents' Sub-Group enhanced parents' confidence and skills.

Sub-groups reported needs and potential solutions to the project board. The project board from this collaboration created a resourced development plan to deliver its goals.

This chapter cannot record the timeline of the growth of THRiVE. Readers are encouraged to visit the website (https://thrivenewtownabbey.co.uk).

Celebrations

- The collaboration developed and brokered a collective funding model. Annually, THRiVE has a budget sourced from health, education, justice, council, voluntary and local funding sources.
- THRiVE's project board developed an agreed provision map and associated five-year plan. This plan champions THRiVE's four priorities.
- THRiVE funded intervention programmes in the local high school and six primary schools are closing attainment gaps for many learners.

- The development of Parent Champions in THRiVE schools is a real inspiration. Parents presenting to THRiVE's project board explain how their involvement has proved to them that as a community, '*we can!*'

- THRiVE has become a well-known brand model for community development across Northern Ireland. Its work fed into the regional *A Fair Start* report.

- In 2022, I had to step away from being chair of THRiVE as I had moved to a role in our regional education authority. Currently, I am assisting in developing a Northern Ireland wide approach to promote schools' collaboration with their communities. The strategy (entitled 'Building Synergy') and its supporting professional learning have been shaped by the experience I gained via the development of THRiVE.

Causation

Why did THRiVE successfully build social capital?

Shared trust

Time was set aside for all participants to build trust. It took over 18 months to bring all stakeholders along, and this often required calculated risk-taking of small steps to bring all on the journey.

Shared purpose

There was a need to continually promote the wider moral responsibility of all participants. This was particularly challenging for the primary schools in the group who were in competition with each other for children. The message was reinforced, however, that '*a rising tide lifts all*'.

Shared expertise

For genuine collaboration all partners are equal. There is no hierarchy of knowledge. In the past, some of THRiVE's participants had endured 'tongue in cheek' assurances that they were valued partners, but the reality was not convincing. What was fundamental to THRiVE's success was the authenticity of engagement with community members as equals to statutory partners.

Michaelangelo, when discussing his art, modestly stated: '*The sculpture is already complete within the marble block before I start my work. It is already there; I just have to chisel away the superfluous material*'.

Effective collaboration is a tool that releases the potential of all when facilitators genuinely trust in the richness of all the participants in their collaboration.

Shared vision

THRiVE's priorities were powerful because members of the community decided them. They recognised that too many people lacked high-enough aspirations and that the community needed to move forward. They owned their journey and maintained control of the improvement pathway.

These priorities were simple and memorable. Steve Jobs' leadership mantra is often quoted: '*Simplicity is the ultimate sophistication*'. When working with many participants it is imperative to keep communication clear and effective.

Shared accountability

THRiVE was egalitarian in its nature but was also a group in which we held others to account. First as a headteacher and then for three years as chair of the THRiVE project board, I was privileged to work with an excellent project leader who was employed via Barnardo's NI to manage THRiVE. She was pivotal in maintaining communication and accountability across the collaboration.

Collaboration is not a means of reducing the need for strong leadership. The opposite is the case. It requires leadership that balances inclusion and decision making effectively without losing the cohesion of the collaboration. *'Democracy is a great idea, but will somebody make a decision'* (Bailie, 2000, p 68).

Shared successes

The project board were delighted when a local PR company donated their services pro bono to help shape and promote its brand. The board were committed to continually share THRiVE's vision. We wanted to create awareness, ownership and a pride in progress being made across the area. Success was celebrated and shared.

Stranmillis University College, Belfast, agreed to be partners of THRiVE. They funded a full-time researcher to help measure the impact of THRiVE's work.

I smile when I pass some local bus shelters and see the six-foot-high THRiVE advertisement. It shows smiling children with their parents. The slogan, very simply, is: *'We Can!'*

Conclusion

I am extremely proud of the work of THRiVE and its impact. Its origins come from a purposeful conversation among a group of invested participants who wanted things to change. With apologies to George Bernard Shaw: *'There are those that look at things the way they are, and ask why? We dreamed of things that never were, and ask why not?'*

 Further reading

Stanford Review Collective Impact Framework (2011). [online] Available at: https://collectiveimpactforum.org/what-is-collective-impact (accessed 3 February 2024).

References

Bailie, F (2000) Research Marketing. Master's dissertation (unpublished). University of Ulster, Belfast.

Department of Education NI (2021) *A Fair Start – Final Report & Action Plan*. [online] Available at: www.education-ni.gov.uk/publications/fair-start-final-report-action-plan (accessed 3 February 2024).

Fullan, M (2014) *The Principal*. San Francisco, CA: Jossey-Bass.

MacGilchrist, B, Reed, J and Myers, K (2004) *The Intelligent School*. 2nd edn. London: Sage Publishing Ltd.

Northern Ireland Assembly (2015) *Tackling Paramilitarism, Criminality and Organised Crime*.

Reason, P (1994) *Participation in Human Inquiry*. London: Sage Publishing Ltd.

Singh, M (1981) Literacy to Development: The Growth of a Tribal Village. In Fermandes, W and Tandon, R (eds) *Participatory Research and Evaluation* (pp 162–71). New Delhi: Indian Social Institute.

The Belfast Agreement (1998). [online] Available at: https://assets.publishing.service.gov.uk/media/619500728fa8f5037d67b678/The_Belfast_Agreement_An_Agreement_Reached_at_the_Multi-Party_Talks_on_Northern_Ireland.pdf (accessed 3 February 2024).

THRiVE (nd). [online] Available at: https://thrivenewtownabbey.co.uk (accessed 3 February 2024).

13 Leading a school to integrated status: bringing about change through persuading, influencing and guiding

ALIX JACKSON

Key learning

- Knowing your 'why' will give you the courage to take the risks needed.

- Leading with moral purpose will energise others to pursue the goal.

- Building trust is critical in times of change. People can't do their best work if they doubt intentions, capabilities, the direction or viability of the change.

AoEA criteria

- Criterion 3. Acting as an enabler by providing support to drive delivery.

- Criterion 4. Enabling knowledge transfer through reference to up-to-date exemplars.

- Criterion 5. Demonstrating authority and professional credibility with clients.

Context

Northern Ireland has arguably one of the most complex educational structures in the world due to the historically divided nature of society. This is reflected in the divided nature of schools themselves, with those identifying as Catholic mainly attending Council for Catholic Maintained Schools (CCMS) and those identifying as Protestant largely attending controlled schools (Montgomery et al, 2003).

Integrated education intentionally brings together pupils, staff and governors from Protestant, Catholic and other religious and cultural traditions within a single school community. As much as a largely segregated education system has prevailed in Northern Ireland, so too has the support for integrated education. In a 2021 LucidTalk poll, 71 per cent of parents stated they would be in favour of integrated education becoming the mainstream education system in Northern Ireland (Johnston, 2021). However, despite the strong appetite for integrated education, only 8 per cent of children in Northern Ireland currently attend integrated schools (Department of Education NI, 2023). While some level of integrated education is available, integrated schools are often oversubscribed and therefore significant numbers of families who desire this type of education cannot access a place. There are also wide areas of Northern Ireland which have yet to establish any integrated provision.

The 1989 Education Reform (Northern Ireland) Order committed the Department of Education to encourage and facilitate the development of integrated education. It also revised a procedure known as transformation, which was originally established in the 1978 Dunleath Act. Transformation allows parents at an existing controlled, maintained or voluntary school to vote to transform it to become an integrated school if certain conditions are met. The 2022 Integrated Education Act also highlights the duty of the Education Authority Northern Ireland (EANI) to encourage, facilitate and support integrated education. There are currently 71 schools which hold integrated status in Northern Ireland. Thirty-one of these schools have become integrated through the transformation process, which has become an important vehicle for the progression of integrated education in Northern Ireland (NICIE, 2023).

Initial exploration

As a Transformation Coordinator for a school who had decided to embark upon this journey, it was vital to understand the detailed requirements of the transformation process, the school's current position and factors which could potentially impact the school in the process. There are several pragmatic reasons schools can pursue transformation, such as falling rolls or threat of closure (McGuinness and Abbot, 2022); therefore, when considering proposals, the Department of Education will evaluate each case very carefully against the following factors:

- **unmet demand for integrated education** in the locality;
- the **sustainability** of the school;
- the **area planning context** and the potential impact on other schools;
- the **religious balance** of the school and the surrounding community;
- evidence of the **planning for transformation**.

In the initial exploration phase the findings demonstrated that there were a range of potential barriers which could impact the Department of Education decision to support transformation for this school.

1. At the time of initiation, the controlled school had a religious balance of:

   - 77.14 per cent Protestant;
   - 2.41 per cent Roman Catholic;
   - 20.45 per cent other religion/no religion.

   Article 92 of the Education Reform (Northern Ireland) Order 1989 states that the Department of Education will not approve a proposal unless reasonable numbers of both Protestant and Catholic pupils are likely to attend the school. Consequently, it would be important to provide compelling evidence on how a more balanced religious school community could be achieved.

2. The religious balance of the board of governors (90 per cent Protestant) meant the board would have to be reconstituted to reflect both the main religious communities more equally.

3. Prior to 2018, the school had experienced negative publicity and unfavourable inspection reports, which had prompted an external intervention and support process by the Education Authority (EA). Under the direction of a new principal in 2018, the school saw significant change in terms of its strategic direction, vision

and ethos (confirmed in an Education and Training Inspectorate (ETI) inspection in 2020). The significant improvement journey the school had already undergone posed the concern that a further large systemic change may be too much, too soon.

Positive drivers

Alongside these challenges it was important to explore and consider the positive drivers that could make for successful change.

1. Information on the enrolment trends and types of neighbouring schools demonstrated that children who identified as Catholic in the locality were travelling a significant distance to attend CCMS schools. In the context of Northern Ireland as a post-conflict society, school ethos is often inextricably linked to culture, identity and community perception of this (Taggart and Roulston, 2022). Unfortunately, due to the community perception of the transforming school as Protestant, the families did not see it as a viable option for their children. The 2011 census data showed that the community surrounding the school was mixed religiously. This demonstrated the potential of achieving a more balanced school community to reflect all sections of the local population and appropriately serve their needs and aspirations.

2. The nearby schools in the locality, including the two closest integrated schools, were oversubscribed; therefore, it was clear that transformation would not have a negative impact on the enrolment of other schools. In fact, transformation would help meet unmet demand for integrated education, as the controlled school was not meeting its enrolment figure and had capacity to welcome additional students.

Taking the information from the initial exploration into account, it was felt that transformation would enable the school to better serve and to reflect the diversity of the wider community, and the findings suggested a transformation bid could be successful against the criteria outlined by the Department of Education. As a result, the board of governors made a formal decision to initiate the transformation process.

A transformation action plan was created to map the vision of the school and evidence how it would work towards transformation over a three-year period. The focus of the plan was to embed the ethos of integrated education throughout the school's governance, curriculum, planning, teaching and learning. Having a clear vision and seeing the long-term goal provided a united purpose and bonded the leaders who would drive this change.

Formal initiation/ballot of parents

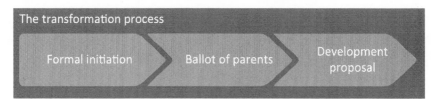

Figure 13.1 The transformation process

Following formal initiation, a school working to transform to integrated status must hold a ballot of parents, who can decide whether or not they feel the school should transform. The ballot, conducted by Civica Electoral Services, must be held no earlier than 28 days and no later than three months from the date of resolution by the board of governors (Department of Education NI, 2017). The decision on whether the transformation process can continue depends entirely on this vote. If the majority of those who vote are in favour, and at least half of those eligible to vote have done so, the board of governors can then submit a development proposal to the Department of Education. However, if these conditions in the ballot are not met, the school cannot continue in the process.

Urgency was key in this phase of the work due to the imposed time constraints and the importance of the parental ballot. A good change message must clearly convey not only the urgency of the action but a sense of confidence that the end goal can be achieved (Dutton and Duncan, 1987). Consulting the school staff and demonstrating the viability of transformation using compelling evidence meant that they wanted to be actively involved in working towards a successful parental ballot.

Often people can believe in the vision but do not mobilise to do the work. While outlining the strategies and plan for staff to engage parents was key, it was so important to speak to the heart (Kotter, 2002). Leaders should never underestimate the power of purpose. Using persuasive leadership strategies, a sense of moral purpose generated an emotional and powerful response from staff. They volunteered their time, making calls to parents encouraging them to vote, holding roadshows in local shopping centres, supporting parental engagement evenings, and giving their time to support question and answer sessions because they believed in the work.

Given the complexity of the education system in Northern Ireland and its links with community culture, the message of transformation was met at times with fear, distrust and cynicism from parents and the wider community. The prevailing question was '*Why?*', '*Why are you doing this?*'; some viewed it as something which was being done 'to' them. The engagement, therefore, had to be both purposeful and incredibly sensitive. It had to be clear that transformation posed no threat, and that parents understood that they were part of the change journey. Building trust and relationship was vital to clearly communicate the sense of opportunity, excitement and purpose of transformation.

The result of the parental ballot, with 62.7 per cent of parents making their vote and 71.1 per cent voting in favour of transformation, was validation of the positive work which had taken place. Governors and staff felt vindicated in the decision to seek transformation, evidenced in the vote of confidence by parents.

Development proposal

The next stage of the process was to create a development proposal (Case for Change) for submission to the Department of Education. This was a collaborative piece of work drawing upon the expertise and advice of the Northern Ireland Council for Integrated Education (NICIE) and EA representatives. It was important to ensure that the momentum gained in the ballot process was not lost while this work was being carried out. Using a model of distributed leadership, a

Transformation Action Group (TAG), made up of key stakeholders, was formed to ensure progress on the transformation action plan continued while the development proposal was being built.

The Case for Change examined and reported on evidence on the unmet demand for integrated education in the locality, the sustainability of the school, the space in the school enrolment and physical environment, the area planning context and the religious balance of the community. It was published in April 2021 for public consultation and provided a compelling case for transformation. In March 2022, the Minister for Education made the decision to approve transformation and the school formally transformed in September 2022.

Conclusion

The transformation journey is fraught with challenges, not only in the conditions imposed by legislation but also in addressing the complex links between the school system and cultural identity. Treating the process with sensitivity is key. Persuasive leadership requires character, vision and the ability to make an emotional connection with those you want to bring with you on the journey. Persuasive leadership can build trust, which becomes the cornerstone to the success of transformation.

While the transformation journey is complex, it has the power to galvanise a whole school community in its widest sense and, in turn, to bring positive change to Northern Ireland's educational landscape and the future for its young people.

 References

Department of Education NI (2017) *Integration Works – Transforming Your School*. [online] Available at: www.education-ni.gov.uk/publicati ons/integration-works-transforming-your-school-guidance (accessed 3 February 2024).

Department of Education NI (2023) Overview of Key Education Statistics. [online] Available at: www.education-ni.gov.uk/sites/default/files/publications/education/School Census Key Statistics 2022.23.pdf (accessed 3 February 2024).

Dutton, J E and Duncan, R B (1987) The Creation of Momentum for Change through the Process of Strategic Issue Diagnosis. *Strategic Management Journal*, 8(3): 279–95.

Integrated Education Act (Northern Ireland) 2022. [online] Available at: www.legislation.gov.uk/nia/2022/15/contents/enacted (accessed 3 February 2024).

Johnston, J (2021) Integrated Education Policy: Where Is the Political Will? [online] Available at: http://qpol.qub.ac.uk/integrated-education-policy-where-is-the-political-will (accessed 3 February 2024).

Kotter, J P (2002) *The Heart of Change: Real-Life Stories of How People Change Their Organizations*. Cambridge, MA: Harvard Business School Press.

McGuinness, S J and Abbott, L (2022) Change Management in Northern Ireland's Transformed Integrated Schools: What We Want is a School Where You Can Be Who You Are and It's a Safe Place. *International Journal of Inclusive Education*, 26(6): 576–91.

Montgomery, A, Fraser, G, McGlynn, C, Smith, A and Gallagher, T (2003) *Integrated Education in Northern Ireland: Integration in Practice*. Coleraine: UNESCO Centre, University of Ulster.

NI Council for Integrated Education (NICIE) (2023) Integrated Schools Today. [online] Available at: https://nicie.org/what-is-integrated-education/integrated-schools-today (accessed 3 February 2024).

Taggart, S and Roulston, S (2022) *School Ethos in Northern Ireland*. Coleraine: UNESCO Centre, University of Ulster.

The Education Reform (Northern Ireland) Order 1989. [online] Available at: www.legislation.gov.uk/nisi/1989/2406/contents (accessed 3 February 2024).

14 Sharing knowledge across the system: building expertise across multiple organisations in support of our most vulnerable young people

DEBI BAILEY

Key learning

- The use of shared language is key. A common or universal language to identify whole family strengths and barriers has enabled a shared understanding and a consistent, holistic approach to working with our most vulnerable young people.

- Deployment of the necessary expertise comes from deep knowledge and understanding of the underlying cause.

- Any work or intervention requires a planned implementation and evaluation. Successful work requires leaders to be able to evaluate the impact (or not) of an approach to supporting sustainable improvement for the individual young person.

AoEA criteria

- Criterion 2. Ability to challenge and work within agreed protocols.

- Criterion 3. Acting as an enabler by providing support to drive delivery.

- Criterion 4. Enabling knowledge transfer through reference to up-to-date exemplars.

Introduction

School leaders are currently experiencing unprecedented challenges. Covid-19 continues to have a significant impact on young people and families, which can be seen in poor mental and physical health. The cost-of-living crisis has compounded issues that our most vulnerable families were already facing, school funding is a significant challenge and there is a recruitment crisis in the sector. Many of these issues are factors in an attendance crisis currently within schools. A recent report into pupil absence, *Listening to, and Learning from, Parents in the Attendance Crisis*, by Dr Sally Burtonshaw and Ed Dorrell (2023) highlights, through the voice of parents, the seismic shift in parental attitudes to both school attendance and, more generally, home and school relationships.

It has never been more important to work in a holistic, multi-agency way as we look to support families, make effective use of the resources available and work to ensure the best possible outcomes for our young people. In this chapter, through detailing an approach to whole trust information and knowledge sharing across sectors, we will draw out some key principles that, when applied, will support the building and development of expertise and ultimately help inform whole family and/or multi-professional working. It will also highlight broader issues for school leaders in relation to impact and the importance of measuring this in a holistic way.

Identifying the cause

As school leaders, we have probably all found ourselves in a situation where we know something is having an impact, but we can't quantify why or we think that an approach is making a difference when in fact it is having no impact whatsoever and when, more often than not, a lack of quality intelligence makes evaluation impossible. This can result in leaders making the wrong decision to continue to implement regardless or indeed to make a decision to initiate a change in approach, both with potentially disastrous consequences. When making strategic decisions, identifying causation so we are able to ensure the right response to achieve the desired outcome is key. In earlier days as a senior leader in a school, I found myself in just this position. We knew our family support worker was having a positive impact on our families, their engagement and ultimately learners' engagement with learning; however, when governors challenged our spending on this role we were unable to quantify and evidence the difference we were making. The family support worker was not able to evidence their own impact and was unable to describe the role in a more strategic way. This led to a journey of development and the implementation of a tool devised to enable the identification and tracking of barriers to learning, and which would support where we needed to take action and affect improvement.

Developing the right framework

Where it was clear that we could not confidently evidence impact of the deployment of key resources within our school, we set about developing an approach that would enable us to measure the success of targeted interventions. The first step was to more precisely understand the challenge we were trying to address. The lack of clear criteria or shared language to describe barriers and levels of vulnerability, aligned with a lack of understanding of the impact barriers were having on learning, was preventing us from the effective deployment of resource and from carrying out any form of impact analysis beyond the anecdotal.

Utilising tools already available (including social care, early help thresholds and the Common Assessment Framework), all key potential barriers to learning were identified including, for example: SEND, attendance, mental health, physical health, behaviour. A criterion by which to assess the level of need and the impact this was having on learning was then developed, ranging from Universal (where no need/barrier is known) to level 4 (where significant barriers and need for impact were identified and where the pupil may have been, for example, a looked after child (LAC), excluded, have complex SEND or significant mental health needs).

Development of a 'windscreen tool' and framework bespoke to our needs

We embraced the concept and developed further the windscreen tool to articulate the level of need, which enabled us to introduce a shared language across our organisation in relation to the impact identified barriers were having on our family, and ultimately, academic outcomes for the learner.

We began initially by mapping a small group of families against the windscreen to ensure we had captured accurately the range of potential barriers and the criteria by which we would measure the impact on a young person and family. This allowed time to review and tweak thresholds and criteria before scaling up and rolling out the application of the windscreen tool across all schools and the mapping of all individual young people against these thresholds.

The windscreen has ensured all professionals across and within the organisation have a shared language when talking about barriers to learning and levels of need. This approach has also helped us to embed a consistent approach to working with families across all of our schools.

Figure 14.1 opposite is a section taken from our windscreen tool.

The effective deployment of resources

Implementation of the windscreen tool led to the development of a 'resource tool' which sits behind the windscreen of need and enables school professionals to access appropriate levels of external support. Developing a simple criteria of need has also enabled the targeted use of resource and makes accountability and responsibility clear because the resource is aligned to specific levels of need, so that within-school staff work with a young person and family up to level 2 on our windscreen. As the use of the windscreen has become more embedded, our schools have been able to more precisely align resource to need, enabling us to make more effective use of funding. A deep knowledge and understanding of our families has enabled a more expert approach to supporting our families. For example, poor mental health was identified as a growing need across all trust schools, as evidenced through the collation of windscreen levels in all of our schools. This helped to evidence the need for the trust to invest in trained counsellors to work with young people because there was real confidence in the identification of need through the use of the windscreen tool.

The indicators can be applied to learners of the wider family. The level of potential vulnerability is a best fit based on all information known about strengths and difficulties.

Factors / Initial indicator of need	EAL / Mobility		PP/FSM / SEND / Red need to be on the tracker.		
	Level 0	Level 1	Level 2	Level 3	Level 4
Capacity	Capacity	School team	School team / Early help / TAS/LIP / Youth worker / SALT	Intensive support/Early help / Central team support / TAS/LIP / Social care / Trust counsellors / Vulnerable learner lead / SALT	Social care / Specialist referrals

Indicator	Level 1	Level 2	Level 3	Level 4
SAFEGUARDING No concerns	In-school support	Early help	CIN / Social care referral	LAC / Child protection
ATTENDANCE at expected 96%+	Below 95% / Occasional non-attendance / Occasional late	90% to 94% / Emerging pattern of non-attendance / Internal truancy / Regular pattern of late	90% and below / PA / Established pattern of non-attendance / Regularly truanting / Significant late	80% and below / Severely absent / NEET / Child not seen / Children missing or running away
BEHAVIOUR Good progress	Occasional prompts needed for work being completed / Lack of progress (1 term) / Lack of engagement	Patterns emerging of inconsistent engagement / School work not completed on time / Sustained lack of progress / PASS indicators	Established behaviour concerns / Regression of progress / Learning significantly impacted / PASS indicators	Complete disengagement with learning / Disrupting the learning for peers
Appropriate / Safe and happy	Victim of bullying / Occasional offending behaviour / Some inappropriate use of social media	Victim of bullying / Emerging pattern of offending behaviour – racist/homophobic / Regular inappropriate use of social media	Anti-social behaviour and/ or racist/ homophobic behaviour which impacts on daily life / Known to YOT / Known to police	Significant issues / Gang activity / Known to YOT / Police involvement
Positive	In year admit / Low level concerns relating to behaviours displayed.	Initial suspension / Emerging pattern of concern	Repeated suspensions / At risk of permanent exclusion / Managed move	Permanent exclusion / FAP admit
Positive relationships	Occasional inappropriate behaviour / Some low-level concerns shared relating to relationships and friendships	Known sexual activity causing concern / Ongoing complaints or shared concerns / Concerns they are vulnerable to exploitation	Sustained known sexual activity / Victim report / Impact on day to day / Evidence they are vulnerable to exploitation	Serious risk of harm / Involved in or at know risk of sexual exploitation

Figure 14.1 Levels of vulnerability and response

As we have developed a common language and criteria in relation to potential barriers to learning, we have also become much more confident and adept at tapping into external agency support because we have a deeper and shared understanding of the need.

Impact on transition

More recently, we have developed further our approach to supporting transition. By applying the windscreen tool, we have been able to identify young people in Years 5 and 6 who are at risk of unsuccessful transition (using the types of criteria we see in FFT Aspire alerts (FFT, 2016) and Public Health England's document on reducing the number of young people not in employment, education and/or training (NEET), including those with special educational needs, receiving free school meals and with low prior attainment (Public Health England, 2016)). We have layered additional information on top of what we already know about the young person and wider family, through the use of an assessment tool which measures pupil attitudes to themselves and learning. This has enabled us to identify a small group of young people who are benefitting from a more bespoke approach. Through the employment of a youth worker, those young people have received weekly intervention in primary school and the youth worker is now supporting those young people into secondary school. While this is another example of an intervention, it is the windscreen tool and the shared language and criteria in relation to vulnerability and barriers to learning that have enabled us to work in this way.

An embedded and digitised system

As the use of the windscreen tool has become embedded, we have developed our strategies and approaches to optimise its use. All schools have a student welfare tracking system, providing a live feed of attendance data, which enables a robust focus on attendance on a daily basis and a joined-up conversation to be held regularly as all information about a young person is held in one place. Our holistic approach is in keeping with the latest Department for Education (2023) guidance around attendance, *Working Together to Improve Attendance*, where the importance of building strong relationships and listening to families to help understand barriers to attendance and working with families to remove them is highlighted. As we have seen a real increase in the barriers to good attendance post-pandemic, through our windscreen tool we have been able to utilise our knowledge and shared understanding of barriers to working in real partnership with our families. A number of additional roles have been developed as a result of all leaders knowing our families well and having real clarity on key barriers to learning. As examples, we have employed a speech and language therapist across our family of schools because the demand was identified through the use of the windscreen tool. We have also created a vulnerable learner lead role to support the effective and consistent application of the windscreen tool across all of our schools. Having a clear reference point in relation to need, which is known and understood by all, has enabled our leaders to utilise the tools to affect system change, improve provision and make a difference. An important part of the role of the vulnerable learner lead is to champion our most vulnerable young people and families and support our schools in planning for and accessing appropriate support.

Dissemination of practice

As a growing trust, we have advised on the implementation of the windscreen tool with other local authorities and organisations tasked with supporting whole family working. We have found the tool to be easily transferrable and that it can be readily utilised as the focus for identifying and addressing potential barriers to learning.

Conclusion

Schools are complex organisations and having a common set of criteria and language to describe a potential barrier and the impact it is having on learning has enabled professionals across and beyond our schools to have a more joined-up approach to supporting our families and vulnerable young people. It has enabled our 'frontline' colleagues to work more smartly. Before the introduction of the windscreen tool, if a school leader had asked a family support worker how many families they were working with, they would have been unable to provide an accurate response because the work was (while impactful in many ways) ad hoc and not necessarily needs driven. Hitherto, many vulnerable young people also 'slipped through the net', while others received intensive support when this may well not have been necessary or appropriate. Our approach to tackling vulnerability has assisted all of our school staff and leaders in becoming knowledgeable in relation to our students' needs and the potential barriers they are experiencing, which in turn has led to a much more holistic, compassionate and successful approach to working with our families.

The windscreen tool and the refining of systems and processes within a coherent framework have enabled our leaders to have an informed understanding of the complexities and realities of life for many of our families across our trust of schools. This means that when we are conversing with other system leaders, providers and partner organisations, we can talk with some authority about the barriers our communities are facing, the difference we are making and address what more needs to be done to affect sustainable improvement for our most vulnerable.

 Further reading

Brummer, J (2020) *Building a Trauma-Informed Restorative School.* London: Jessica Kingsley Publishers.

Education Endowment Foundation (2019) *Putting Evidence to Work – A School's Guide to Implementation*. [online] Available at: https://educationendowmentfoundation.org.uk/education-evidence/guidance-reports/implementation (accessed 3 February 2024).

Education Endowment Foundation (nd) Wider Strategies. [online] Available at: https://educationendowmentfoundation.org.uk/support-for-schools/school-planning-support/3-wider-strategies (accessed 3 February 2024).

References

Burtonshaw, S and Dorrell, E (2023) *Listening to, and Learning from, Parents in the Attendance Crisis*. [online] Available at: www.schoolhomesupport.org.uk/wp-content/uploads/2023/09/Listening-to-and-learning-from-parents-in-the-attendance-crisis.pdf (accessed 3 February 2024).

Department for Education (2023) *Working Together to Improve School Attendance*. [online] Available at: www.gov.uk/government/publications/working-together-to-improve-school-attendance (accessed 3 February 2024).

FFT (2016) *FFT Aspire Alerts*. [online] Available at: https://help.fft.org.uk/wp-content/uploads/FFT_Aspire_Student_Explorer_KS2.pdf (accessed 3 February 2024).

Public Health England (2016) *Local Action on Health Inequalities: Reducing the Number of Young People Not in Employment, Education or Training (NEET)*. [online] Available at: https://assets.publishing.service.gov.uk/media/5a7dd2a040f0b65d88634a03/Review3_NEETs_health_inequalities.pdf (accessed 3 February 2024).

15 Building a community of generous, effective leaders

KAREN BRAMWELL

Key learning

- Acting as an enabler, to build a community of collaborative, generous leaders in the context of a multi-academy trust through the use of a 'social contract' that supports deep relationships and trust in one another.

- Empowering headteachers in the multi-academy trusts to act as 'cultural architects' through modelling values and practices vital to the organisation.

- The benefits of being outward looking and seeking out opportunities for knowledge transfer through involvement in wider system approaches.

AoEA criteria

- Criterion 1. Demonstrating personal attributes and skills.

- Criterion 3. Acting as an enabler by providing support to drive delivery.

- Criterion 4. Enabling knowledge transfer through reference to up-to-date exemplars.

- Criterion 5. Demonstrating authority and professional credibility with clients.

An introduction to Forward As One

Forward As One is a growing and successful Church of England, multi-academy trust (MAT) of 13 primary schools situated in five different local authorities in the Greater Manchester region. Forward As One grew from a successful, inner-urban, multi-cultural, National Support School (NSS) with a role to share practice with others to raise the quality of education in schools that were experiencing difficulty. Being a Church of England MAT means we also follow the Church of England's 'Vision for Education'; our work is rooted in Christian values that are the heart of all that we do.

Initially, the name of the trust was that of the founding school. However, this didn't feel representative of us as trust leaders; we therefore renamed the trust 'Forward As One'. We feel this name exemplifies exactly what we do: we move forward together – as one. We consider that collectively we are as strong as our weakest school – if one fails, we all fail. Thus, our ethos is one of collective accountability and collaboration – we are '*One Team, One Mission, One Family*'. It is our '*One Mission*' to be '*One Team*' where everyone can flourish because we believe that when adults flourish, the children flourish too.

> *Flourishing is the product of the pursuit and engagement of an authentic life that brings inner joy and happiness through meeting goals, being connected with life passions, and relishing in accomplishments through the peaks and valleys of life.*
>
> (Soots, nd)

We are 100 per cent Ofsted graded 'Good' or better, having moved three schools from 'Inadequate' to 'Good', one of which we transformed from 'Requires Improvement' to 'Good' and another issued with a local authority warning notice to 'Good'. Some of the schools that we have been supporting as a MAT were previously judged as less than 'Good' for over a decade.

Among my many roles as trust leader, I see that of acting as an enabler by providing support to drive delivery to be one of the most important. Creating the mechanisms through which delivery of support can be instrumented has been a key driver. Nurturing the culture of the organisation involves creating a climate of mutual respect. It is a joy to now see professionals sharing ideas, giving and receiving challenges, and orchestrating the forward movement of thinking.

How do you build a community of collaborative, generous leaders?

My work supporting dozens of schools across the north-west of England taught me the importance of 'contracting' at the beginning of any professional relationship, ensuring that protocols are clearly understood by both parties, and that challenge is to be expected and encouraged on both sides. A large part of the success in helping others to lead has been built on mutual trust, professional respect and the professional credibility that arises from a track record of successful leadership in challenging schools. I am always conscious of the importance of ensuring that the impact of my leadership as both a school leader and a MAT leader must stand up to scrutiny for me to be able to advise others credibly.

As a leader, I have been influenced by the work of Professor David Hargreaves on system leadership (Hargreaves, 2012); alongside his work on the creation of deep partnerships, effective joint practice development and the importance of developing a collective moral purpose. When the trust was born, I was determined that our partnership would move well beyond the 'shallow' and into the 'deep' and 'tight' quadrants that Figure 15.1 illustrates.

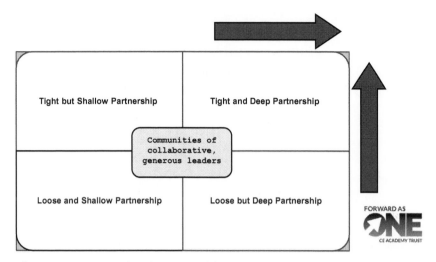

Figure 15.1 Inter-school partnerships

The approach we have developed is to work through a series of '*Learning and Leading Communities*' on '*Trust Tuesdays*'. These are the key conduit for joint practice development for us. Our 'communities' are made up of leaders from different schools who undertake the same role, for example a curriculum leader for science or special needs. The 'communities' are held in person or online, and always take place every Tuesday so that cover can be arranged to relieve leaders from their teaching commitments.

Our headteachers collaborate to determine agreed objectives/ outcomes for each learning community. This is agreed in our weekly KIT (Keeping in Touch) meetings, which are online and therefore largely for information-sharing purposes, and our half-termly Headteacher Thinktank meetings, which are collaborative learning and decision-making events.

Headteachers as cultural architects

It is our strongly held belief that it is the school leader who 'creates the weather' in their school. They are the banner holder for our organisation – the cultural architects (Hughes, 2018) – constantly influencing attitudes within their school. It is therefore absolutely vital that they understand the purpose and thinking that sits behind our approach – they need to understand why we operate the way we do. The approach that we have taken in response to this is to get to know our leaders well (with depth), understand what drives them, and identify their individual strengths and preferred methods of working.

To do this, within our Headteacher Thinktank, we use various tools that support the individuals' understanding of themselves, utilising the group situation to support their understanding of each other. The group dynamics here are especially important. It has become increasingly important for this to be done at 'growth points' as we welcome new members to the team. Growth points occur when new schools join our organisation – for instance, in 2022, three schools joined the MAT at the same time. This increased the membership of our 'communities' by a third (from 9 to 12), which necessitated a revisit of our 'contracting', building new relationships with the changes in group dynamics. They need to be able to understand themselves as well as others with whom they work closely.

Social contracting

Through this process we have learned that some of our best thinkers are very reflective and therefore unlikely to share their best ideas when in a situation where they are asked for an immediate response; thus, this has influenced how we structure the meetings.

Before the Covid-19 pandemic, we had started to use online meetings as a tool due to the travelling distances between our schools. When we moved to wholly online meetings in 2020, it was even more important that the sense of community and trust within our network was strong. This new way of working and our journey of growth have taught us the importance of putting a social contract in place. It is vital that our staff are 'present' – that they 'turn up' in both body and mind. Their attendance at these communities is important to their colleagues as they are there to support the development of their school, that of others and the trust as a whole. We make this explicit before new members join and now start each meeting with a reminder of 'why we are here' – of the horizontal accountability that we are aiming for.

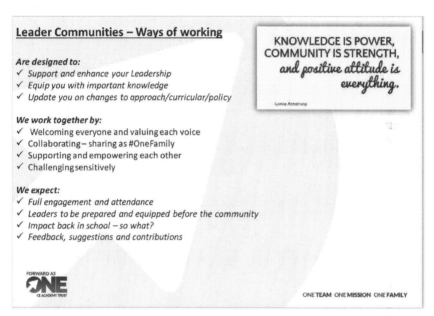

Figure 15.2 Our social contract

As can be seen in Figure 15.2, expectations of attendance and responsibility towards each other, as well as engagement in learning for themselves, their schools and each other are clear. Headteachers are the leaders of learning within their organisation: they understand the purpose of the meeting for each community because they collaborate to determine the foci; all materials and outcomes are available for them to access (pre and post meeting) so that the learning, expectations of staff and follow-up activities in school are explicit and can be actioned effectively in school.

Communities often start with a 'think piece' (up-to-date exemplars used to enable knowledge transfer) to familiarise staff with the topic (the expectation that all members of the group will engage with this think piece is clear). Then, further learning and discussion takes place in the meeting either online or face to face. The inclusion of a think piece, or another activity prior to the meeting, is deliberately designed to gain the most from those people who need to reflect in order to formulate their ideas. By operating like this, it is our aim to 'flip learning' so that staff take responsibility for their own development as professionals. I have been delighted at how well our staff engage with these activities as they arrive at the learning community empowered to share their ideas.

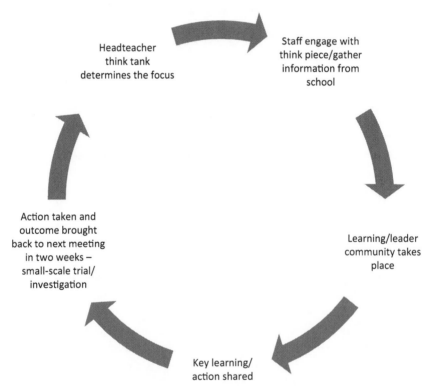

Figure 15.3 Cycle of engagement and action

The timing of our wider learning communities is also of significant importance. We made the decision to have them at the same time every week so that each school could ensure that staff have quality release time in which to engage in their professional development. We determine whether to hold the meeting online or in person dependent upon the content, as we are aiming to minimise staff workload and our carbon footprint by limiting travel times. Meetings are timed to work as a series of meetings which go through a sequence of learning and involve intersessional activity back in school. It is imperative that school leaders are in accordance with this, as time must be given for staff to engage in follow-up activities.

Trust is a vital element of these communities too. We aim to create the conditions in which this can happen by modelling positive behaviours. Staff understand that we are there to support one another – that this is a safe place in which to share their work, pupil work and data. Members who have participated in these groups for some time are champions of this way of working, drawing in new members to build their confidence up.

As a group of schools, we are determined to avoid becoming an echo chamber of our own ideas. We therefore engage in networks and activities beyond our trust which take place locally and nationally and, to a more limited extent, internationally.

The Aspire Hub: looking up, out and beyond

In order to continue to look beyond Forward As One, we partnered with another trust in the north-west to create a Challenge Partners Hub – The Aspire Hub (Challenge Partners is an educational charity with a national presence describing itself as 'a national Network of Excellence'). This Hub has been established using a similar approach – creating a social contract collaboratively with a strong sense of 'why'. The Aspire Hub prides itself on being a network wherein everyone is prepared to 'Look Up, Out and Beyond' – utilising and drawing upon the expertise of the Challenge Partners national network (which is a network of over 500 schools). The social contract was codified by the founding group in 2019 around three core principles: collaboration, culture and connectedness.

A culture of collaboration, not competition, was central to the success of this partnership ('culture'). Considering the variety and contexts of schools within the Hub, two different trusts alongside local authority maintained schools, it was imperative that colleagues subscribed to this culture of support and challenge – in essence, that they connected with each other and felt sufficiently secure to be vulnerable. An example of this is a question we often reflect on in our 'temperature check' agenda item of '*What is currently keeping you awake at night?*' thus modelling the importance of supporting and empowering each colleague to lean on the group as/when needed ('connectedness'). Finally, collaboration is emphasised – the expectation that the group will contribute and be active partners, not passive ones, and that each school leader is responsible for contributing to the learning of others ('collaboration' principle).

Final reflections

During my journey as a leader, I spent a short period working within a local authority school improvement team. An issue that was raised repeatedly was '*How do we reach those schools that are disengaged?*'. Experience had shown us that those schools who opted out, who didn't attend, were often struggling. Their non-attendance was frequently the first sign of their struggle. Returning to David Hargreaves' (2012) work on the self-improving school system, these schools were 'islands' – sometimes 'Outstanding', other times struggling – the thing these 'islands' have in common is their lack of accountability or relationship with others. This is why we have attempted to design our communities so that they are:

- relevant;
- realistic;
- consistent;
- co-designed;

- collaborative;

- comfortable;

- non-threatening.

Through our communities, which are our main point of weekly contact with all of our schools, we constantly reinforce our trust values:

- family – working together for collective success;

- openness – sharing with, and being accountable to, others;

- resilience – overcoming challenges through commitment and perseverance;

- wisdom – a life-long love for learning, understanding the world around us;

- aspiration – pursuing excellence in all that we do;

- research – grounding everything we do in evidence and best practice;

- diversity – fostering inclusive and vibrant learning communities.

Through constant reinforcement and implementation of our trust values we have enabled our development of a self-improving school system within the MAT itself.

We do not see our learning communities as a luxury or an add-on; they are a key tool in our strategy to keep our schools moving 'Forward As One'. It is therefore important that schools have the release time for the staff identified at the beginning of the year, every Tuesday afternoon. This investment in our staff has proved substantially beneficial.

We are also a growing trust – learning as we go. We need to determine the optimum group size and identify whether we should have synchronous meetings in geographical hubs so that we can have more meetings face to face while minimising the need to travel. As with everything, we will undertake some small-scale trials and make the decision collaboratively with our staff.

Conclusion

In summary, we have created a series of communities of effective leaders, underpinned by the strength of a shared social contract, supported by generous, effective school leaders who have deep relationships with, and responsibility for, one another. All of our schools have improved. Those who joined as strong, 'converter' schools and those who joined when experiencing difficulty or deemed 'failing' are all now graded 'Good' or above by Ofsted. It is clear that our method of school improvement has enabled major transformation. The staff (the majority of whom were there when the schools were graded inadequate) are empowered and continually developing and are now strong practitioners and leaders making a positive difference to the lives of pupils. Through education we rise!

 References

Hargreaves, D (2012) *A Self-improving School System: Towards Maturity*. Cambridge: Wolfson College.

Hughes, D (2018) *The Barcelona Way: Unlocking the DNA of a Winning Culture*. London: Macmillan.

Soots, L (nd) Flourishing. *The Positive Psychology People*. [online] Available at: www.thepositivepsychologypeople.com/flourishing (accessed 3 February 2024).

16 Transform your school the hard, slow and satisfying way

MIKE BUCHANAN

Key learning

- All too frequently, it is feelings which are the driver of people's behaviours and a key role of the adviser is to enable those with whom we work to discern between fact and feeling.

- Clarity of purpose within a climate of trust are powerful ingredients in engaging people in a process of change.

- In affecting change, evidence and agree the focus with simplicity and transparency.

- Altering people's behaviours and enabling sustainable change takes time and patience. It is a slow though satisfying way to engage those with whom we work in the process of continuous improvement.

AoEA criteria

- Criterion 1. Demonstrating personal attributes and skills.

- Criterion 2. Ability to challenge and work within agreed protocols.

- Criterion 3. Acting as an enabler by providing support to drive delivery.

Introduction

I have come late in life to the writings of Maya Angelou, the American poet and civil rights activist. I rather regret it. One of her more memorable quotes is: '*I've learned that people will forget what you said, people will forget what you did, but people will never forget how you made them feel*'.

In my experience of school leadership, advising and executive coaching so far, it's the feelings which are most often the driver for behaviours and performance, even if they remain unacknowledged. One of our aims as an adviser is to improve individual and organisational performance by helping people to see the facts and understand the feelings – their own and those of others.

One recent August, while enjoying the warmth of the summer sun in the tranquil peace of our Kent garden, I received a call asking if I might be interested in an interim headship starting in a few days' time. While I have decades of experience as a school leader and am active professionally as a strategic consultant and coach, I was not really looking for such a role. Nonetheless intrigued, I asked about the role and the school, and why I was the person they called. It turned out I already knew the school and the role was a 12-month change project to realign the school ready for a new head. Now this excited me as I could see how I might be able to add some value.

Formulating an initial hypothesis

The fundamentals at the school were sound if not secure. The pupils were, on the whole, happy and wished to be at the school. Academic outcomes were good overall and the pupils had some opportunities for personal development. Crucially for a fee-paying school, the market for future recruitment was clearly defined. The employees were committed and loyal. So, what were the issues which meant it was faltering and change was needed?

Before agreeing to take on the role of interim head, I asked to have a conversation with the governors as I wanted to better understand their perspective or, as it turned out, perspectives. I met with two pairs of governors and simply asked them to tell me about the school. During one conversation, the pair talked over each other and were at odds with each other for an hour. During the second conversation, one of the governors talked to me about the future of the school and painted an enticing picture of possibilities, while the other talked about debilitating operational financial matters which would make such possibilities a pipe dream. Now I knew I could add value and that there was at least one person with a vision for the future.

The school is young and still had many of the characteristics of a 'start-up'. Like many start-ups, the original founders, as represented by the governors, are extremely committed to the original purpose but a mature, formal governance structure was slow to emerge. Some policies and processes had not kept up with the growth of the school, the demands of the market or organisational effectiveness. There were many committed and loyal employees who wished to contribute to the future success of the school. Often they were working hard with varying degrees of efficacy as a result of a lack of clarity of purpose and coordination. Evaluation of impact was not systematic. Where a vacuum existed, it was often filled by those who happened to be interested even if this was not their remit or strength. The result was that there was much unfocused activity, many uncoordinated systems, gaps and people inefficiently deployed.

Like many organisations, this school had lost its way and issues that should have been addressed had been ignored, sidestepped or put in the 'too hard' box by successive combinations of governors and executives. Dysfunctional governance and leadership had become the norm with governors often acting unilaterally and operationally, thereby disempowering the leadership of the school.

Establishing, with staff and governors, clarity of purpose and role

My starting point was to clarify what it was we were trying to achieve in each area and gain agreement about this; to simplify our approach so that we had consistency and coherence; and to enable the people best placed to lead, manage and implement while removing barriers and providing resources for them to be successful. Clarity of roles, responsibility, resources and authority alongside expectations of outcomes and behaviours was the starting point for sustained success, as a lack of clarity was often the source of frustration and inaction.

People flourish, and organisations thrive, when they experience a balance of positive emotions, engagement with the world, good relationships with others, a sense of meaning and moral purpose, and the accomplishment of valued goals. My aim is to enable those around me to flourish and to live joyous, fulfilled lives even in the face of great challenge. This grand purpose drives everything in my professional and personal lives. What's your purpose?

So, clarify, simplify and enable became the mantra for future success. Most organisations layer complexity on complexity because it is easy to do. Our role as advisers is to strip back and simplify so that people might see clearly for themselves.

Keep it simple

Schools should be 'simple' organisations within which to work. Distilled to its finest level, schools have two purposes or reasons to exist: to maximise the achievements of children and to develop them as people so that they may flourish as adults.

The elements that I have come to look for and that I believe make up thriving schools, which are successful in powering these two purposes, are:

- attitudes = values learned and expressed through behaviours;

- achievements = broad and deep (not merely focused on examinations) – these re-energise the values and attitudes, and re-enforce positive behaviours;

- agency = children and young people who act to improve their worlds to elevate happiness and eliminate misery – this gives meaning;

- knowledge = understanding in depth is a power amplifier;

- networks = local, regional, national and international – supportive people who power up happiness and drain misery away;

- ethics = living life in the service of others and with humility;

- well-being = based on individual character strengths and needs;

- skills = including knowing how to ask great questions and having the courage to ask them.

Again, delivery of these elements should be 'simple' and typically involves:

- good teaching by experts in the subject and in how children learn;
- expert leadership by all that builds a positive climate, and a culture of challenge and calculated risk-taking;
- a professional focus on maximising the achievements of pupils and developing others.

Evidence the need for change with total transparency

As we know, change, if not the uncertainty which comes with it, is welcomed by some and feared by others. Establishing an open and frank, evidence-informed dialogue with all within the organisation so that they are well informed and understand the reasoning for change is paramount, appreciated and helps to minimise uninformed speculation and unproductive gossip. In engaging others in change, it is helpful to avoid 'either/or' thinking and promote 'both/and' attitudes. Questioning, which for some may suggest doubt about the nature of what has gone before, is designed to prompt thinking and imagine possibilities. Understanding too that the need for change is not something with which all will immediately connect means that there may be a period of learning and acclimatisation to be undergone. The priorities, in this case, as the catalyst of change, were in challenging and supporting staff, and in the establishment of effective systems to enable improvement.

With around 100 school days tenure as interim head remaining after an initial period of work within the school, the aim was to ensure the new head was well placed to start in the following September. In this case, informed by the evidence gathering, the focus was on:

- supporting effective governance, which would help to provide direction, oversight, support and productive challenge by developing a framework for a five-year plan;
- taking a step towards a meticulous, effective, sustainable business;
- making some immediate, symbolic, strategic investments in facilities and people;

- undertaking a curriculum realignment to increase teaching time and unlock further opportunities for improving the pupil experience in areas such as sport, PSHE, activities and the academic curriculum.

As with most successful change processes, while the school is now more strongly placed to move forward, the gain wasn't entirely without pain, and it has a permanent head with the skills, vision and energy to help the school with its reinvigorated staff to build on what has been done and to thrive.

In reflecting on this intervention, the following will undoubtedly chime with others' experiences.

The importance of culture

A school culture which focuses primarily on summary judgements of employees' performance, punitive control and narrow accountability measures is unlikely to build or sustain continuing high esteem or performance. On the other hand, establishing a positive culture of open reflection and analysis almost certainly will.

Listen, listen and listen again

Most of us are great talkers and even if we take the time to listen to others, it's too often so that we can respond to what they are saying as quickly as possible – just like snatching a ball from someone else so that we can play with it. One of the hardest things to achieve as an adviser when the pressure is on is to listen, to really listen and maybe to listen again so that you can work out what the underlying facts and feelings really are. Only by listening carefully can you hope to understand fully and then help to enable the person you are advising to take responsibility for the changes in behaviours needed to improve.

Not everyone is 'achievement' driven to the same extent

McCelland's Theory of Needs suggests everyone has three motivators that need to be satisfied across their personal and professional lives: achievement, affiliation and power/influence (Kurt, 2021). People behave very differently according to how well their needs in each of these areas are being satisfied. Indeed, many of the 'problems' arise as a result of there being a mismatch between one of these needs and the ability of the person to have it fulfilled or not. As an adviser, discerning the individual's need or key driving instinct may well be key in changing an individual's mindset.

Percolated coffee has so much more depth of flavour but it takes time

Instant coffee is, well, 'instant' and it has little lasting flavour or satisfaction. Barista coffee can be tedious to prepare but so much more satisfying. The same can be true of advising. It can take time for people, for a multitude of reasons, to achieve a depth of understanding that helps them to commit and see a way forward. Ultimately, it is much more satisfying to achieve that engagement and sometimes we just have to be patient. A 'quick return' can come at a cost but, moreover, it's great to enjoy the aroma of the coffee as it percolates through the minds of the people we advise and lead.

How many times can you ask the same question?

Just like the best learning in lessons, some of the best advising can require a person being advised to suffer cognitive fatigue as a result of thinking long and hard about the issues. Asking the right questions in a number of ways enables individuals to explore, evaluate, summarise and synthesise. Effective advice often entails finding different ways of asking the same open-ended question. These questions might be prompted by a discussion of a model, data, people or other ways of breaking the thinking down into manageable and digestible pieces.

The light-bulb moment can lead to transformation

There is often a moment or moments of revelation: the light-bulb moment. Most often, this occurs when people realise or finally acknowledge that they can transform their circumstances by taking more collective or individual responsibility for their actions, the way they behave and the way they engage with others. Realising that they have control over such matters and options for the future is often a moment of great emotion – be ready for it and let it happen.

Discern between fact and feeling

Barriers to change can too often be relational. In such circumstances, the feelings of individuals can remain hidden for some time, but they are nearly always the driver of behaviours and so they have to be sought out and addressed. In other words, both the emotional and the rational have to be at the core of advising as all people are somewhere along the spectrum from one to the other.

Conclusion

The purpose of advising is to improve both personal and organisational performance so that our children and young people achieve to their optimum. Great advising is demanding of both the adviser and those engaging with the advice. Change only becomes transformation when it is sustained and demonstrated by the behaviours of people, which takes time to become truly embedded.

Transformation is slow, hard but ever so satisfying!

 References

Angelou, M (nd). [online] Available at: www.thesuccessfulspirit.com/maya-angelou-people-will-forget/ (accessed 8 February 2024).

Kurt, S (2021) McClelland's Three Needs Theory: Power, Achievement, and Affiliation. [online] Available at: https://educationlibrary.org/mcclellands-three-needs-theory-power-achievement-and-affiliation (accessed 8 February 2024).

17 Organising change in changing organisations

DAME KATHY AUGUST

Key learning

- In the advisory role, it is important for there to be authenticity in purpose, values and people.

- Ethical considerations impact on people in various ways.

- Advisers can work constructively with partners through establishing clear and flexible parameters for their work.

AOEA criteria

- Criterion 1. Demonstrating personal attributes and skills.

- Criterion 2. Ability to challenge and work within agreed protocols.

- Criterion 3. Acting as an enabler by providing support to drive delivery.

- Criterion 5. Demonstrating authority and professional credibility with clients.

Change is a process, not an event: supporting a leadership transition

This chapter describes my role in assisting a governing body in supporting the induction of an existing executive leader into the most senior role in the organisation. This required support to enable their establishment in the role. Successful 'landing' depended on managing the dynamics of the team around them, including the real sense of bereavement at the 'loss' of the previous very popular and dynamic leader. A number of staff and governors were increasingly anxious that as the leadership changed the trust might roll back to the dysfunction that existed prior to the exiting leader arriving. Ensuring that the transition was as smooth as possible and accelerating the learning of the new leader was essential to protect progress.

In this instance the most prominent criteria in play were acting as an enabler by providing support to drive delivery and demonstrating authority and professional credibility. The context was such that there was a temptation for the adviser to 'morph' into being an interim executive leader. This would have been a mistake for all stakeholders. The work called for clarity surrounding the adviser role and scope, how this was articulated and how it would look in practice. Fidelity to what was negotiated was essential, as was the recognition that if unexpected situations arose flexibility would be needed. Pivoting in small ways from an agreed way of operating should not be problematic providing the working relationship that has been established is strong and underpinned by mutual trust.

Context

A small trust which had been in operation for just over five years had made rapid improvement after a disappointing start. It had been expected that the chief executive leader, credited with the transformation would remain in post for a few years longer and not leave until improvement was fully sustainable. The news that the CEO had been headhunted for a new post and was leaving left the MAT in shock. The board, leadership team, staff, students and the community served by the trust had invested in the CEO and there was a collective mourning at the news of the departure. The organisation's transformation was seen as being due to their leadership alone. This led to a legitimate fear that any crisis of confidence at the departure would overwhelm and reverse the progress made. Despite this the board had agreed to the CEO leaving early. This was to enable the replacement to be appointed for the summer term and ensure the new academic year would be uninterrupted with interviews and appointments.

The decision had caused some disquiet with other trustees but strategically it was a sound one. It ensured the new academic year would have an uninterrupted focus on the classroom and provision. Not only would the new academic year have an uninterrupted focus, it would also reduce the period of 'limbo leadership', ie of a leader in role but waiting to leave and decisions delayed for the new postholder.

There was an internal candidate who was the preferred choice but who had limited experience. The chair and the board considered appointing an interim executive to operate as a part-time CEO, with the CEO's potential replacement fulfilling the role of operational CEO reporting to the interim executive.

This was the position when the chair approached an adviser with the intention of them fulfilling this interim role.

Stage 1: introduction (analyse and explain)

The first conversation with the chair questioned the proposal and the rationale behind it. It became apparent that the rationale for the view was based on their perception that what they had been told about the organisation was absolute as they had been told it by the departing CEO. This was not misleading but the board was in danger of trying to artificially maintain the leadership unchanged and in the image of the previous CEO. The single-prism view limited vision and the board needed support to see the change as an opportunity for further growth. New leadership does bring risks but risks that can be mitigated and controlled. The professional challenge for the adviser was to help the board understand how to mitigate the risk and how their work as an adviser would assist. The approach needed to protect progress made from any reversal but not neuter the new leader or create confusion for stakeholders. Both of these were dangers which could imperil further improvement and the reputation of the organisation.

This balance was achieved by the adviser by drawing on previous similar experiences and sharing outcomes of those case studies with the chair. In this instance, it was important that the adviser maintain their objectivity and emotional detachment to avoid shifting position from advising to persuading. The language used in such conversations is important. Boards should have a balanced skill set and many have experienced professionals as trustees or directors. Some will have as much or more experience as advisers with issues such as change management. Not all will appreciate the dynamics in educational settings, however, which is why metaphor and analogy as linguistic devices can be put to good use to make the point effectively.

Being cognisant of a board's skill mix is helpful, but the adviser is operating within a very specific context, and this gives the role the distinction among the group of professionals.

The success of advisory work is often less about 'episodic victories', although they do play a role, and more about the longer view of incremental steps that produce sustained progress (Gawande, 2017). An adviser needs to be comfortable with their contribution to improvement seeming to be almost peripheral as opposed to central to the project in hand.

Stage 2: learn (absorb and appreciate)

The agreement with the chair and trustees and the willing acceptance by the promoted executive leader was the beginning of the adviser's input. It is very useful for all parties if the agreement includes a reporting method. In some cases there will be an end-of-project report. In others, interim reports on aspects of the work may be needed. In the case of this commission there were a number of interim progress reports provided. For the board these were delivered in person so as to enable questioning of the evaluative element. The next action was to find out enough about the organisation for the advisory task to have purchase and impact.

A brief introduction at the start of a full staff meeting ensures that everyone knows who the adviser is and what the scope of the role is. Staff want and need to know about the professional credibility of advisers but they don't need a grandstanding presentation. If any adviser infers they are on a 'rescue mission', the professional relationship will suffer and the confidence of the staff team will be damaged. Establishing professional positive working relationships framed the piece of work. It helped the confidence of staff that the role of the adviser would help bring a degree of protection from the instability that can result from a change in leadership. Care had to be taken to avoid the framing to be twisted out of shape by allowing the relationship to become too 'cosy' or familiar. This would have devalued the work of the adviser by threatening a reduced objectivity and over-emphasise the participant part of the 'observer participant' role which all those undertaking advisory work fulfil. Using this fact-finding or orientation period helped to ensure that time was not wasted and advice was properly targeted and bespoke.

Returning to advice given by building in a feedback loop for stakeholders, allows them time for processing the impact of the change. This helped remove any misunderstandings that might have arisen as a result of the constant development of the language surrounding education, which when used carelessly can create confusion.

Stage 3: complete and finish

The move to the final stage of the commission began once a realistic picture of the organisation, its people, coverage and gaps, strengths and weaknesses had formed. A conscious effort was needed to avoid the danger of assuming that what was now clear to the adviser about the needs and priorities of the organisation was equally obvious to those being advised. The adviser's 'diagnosis' was based on being present and observing but was also informed by significant professional experience and skills honed by practice. This practical wisdom or phronesis by definition cannot be assumed.

This third stage was when the original agreement was revisited and reviewed along with the observations, findings and evaluations made to form the final report to the board. On this occasion the senior leader fulfilling the operational CEO role was appointed to the substantive role. This was after an interview process in which the CEO was said to have shown considerable professional growth and increased confidence.

In this last stage there is the need for what might best be described as a tapering or exit strategy. The adviser's view was that the more effective they had been, the less they would be needed. If the commission is successful, the improvements in the school or college are owned by the people in it.

Included in the final reports produced was a series of suggested further actions for consideration. The word '*suggested*' is deliberate. These were not listed as 'Recommendations' or 'Points for Action' as these can create an 'audit' impression to what then follows. To paraphrase a quote which has been heard regularly recently: '*The adviser advises, (others) decide*'.

The tapering or exit strategy began when the advisory commitment tapered from one day per week to one day per fortnight for a month, moving to one day per month until the end of the term. After this, there was an opportunity to make contact by phone with a follow-up face-to-face visit after a term if the board or CEO made that request.

After six months, a 'keeping in touch' email was sent by the adviser with a simple message. Invariably such KIT messages are very well received and it is a reminder to colleagues that when times are challenging there are people who they can ask for help and that these are professionals who are tried, tested and trusted.

Conclusion

In this process the adviser was the enabler: it required confidence in the midst of uncertainty that stems from phronesis (deep professional wisdom rooted in experience). As the piece of advisory work draws to a close, its value should be evident: in the increased confidence of leaders, the stability of people and place and in this case specifically the understanding of the board. With this came the realisation that the adviser role was no longer needed for this particular issue. The more successful a piece of advisory work has been, the less noticeable should be the role of the adviser who enabled it.

Further reading

Hamaya, S and Oya, T (2013) Phronetic Leaders: Designing New Business, Organization and Society. *Fujitsu Science Technology Journal*, 49(1): 402–6.

Parkinson, C N (1958) *Parkinson's Law, or The Pursuit of Progress*. London: John Murray.

 Reference

Gawande, A (2017) The Heroism of Incremental Care. *The New Yorker*, 15 January.

Conclusions: reflections on Book 1, *The Role of the Education Adviser*

DR TONY BIRCH AND IAN LANE

Our belief is that all children, teachers and leaders want to improve; we seek to promote a culture in which support and challenge are welcomed and dependence on external compliance and regulation is reduced.

AoEA

Throughout this book, the influence and impact of the education adviser has been illustrated and demonstrated and their repertoire of approaches made visible. It is optimistic in recognising that contributions to a self-improving system (Hargreaves, 2012) come from a range of sources, where a professional collective responsibility is brought to bear, where expertise is valued above ideology and where responsibility for improvement emerges according to need – as Eric Halton's chapter describes this, skilled advisers work in 'concert'.

The thinking of Professor Dame Alison Peacock in England and Mary Lowery in Northern Ireland both provide insight into how advisers can positively influence an education system and Professor Andy Hargreaves gives us a more expansive view in his international context.

Demonstrating personal attributes and skills

As the chapters have unfolded, the range of personal attributes and skills needed by the education adviser have been revealed. This is always in part a response to context but also a result of the experiences, expertise and approaches that characterise skilled advisers. First and foremost, relational skills emerge as a feature in every example presented here: however, they depend too on advisers whose credibility is forged in addressing the pressing need they see in front of them with purpose and flexibility.

We see the necessary repertoire in the chapters by Eithne Leming and Martyn Beales: they represent the self-awareness and reflectiveness that underpin the adviser's attributes and skills. This ability to build rapport and communicate powerfully are at the heart of the *'supportive intervention'* which Les Walton calls for in Chapter 6.

Ability to challenge and work within agreed protocols

In the commissions and activities undertaken by advisers, attuning to the client is an essential ability of the effective adviser. A laser-like focus on what needs to be done is often coupled with an ability to understand what is at the heart of the issue (an understanding of causality, for example). Through this comes challenge: the ability to skilfully analyse what is needed for change to take place and through dialogue creating both an understanding and an appetite to address challenges. The chapters by both Tom Grieveson and Kevin McDermid remind us that a key part of the effectiveness of the adviser is to understand this role and that it will vary from context to context: defining scope and being clear about impact are vital in any deployment of advisers, individual or collective.

Acting as an enabler by providing support to drive delivery

Without impact, the adviser risks criticism: their ability to support and enable change lies at the heart of their work. Whether working individually or with others, creating a powerful combination of energy and capacity emerges as a key skill. While this draws out the capacities of the client, it also involves connecting to others, brokering expertise and enabling collaboration across organisations.

Multi-academy trust chief executives Debi Bailey and Karen Bramwell illustrate how they have, through generosity of spirit and a clear focus, enabled others to respond to challenges. There is a similar theme in the chapters by Mike Buchanan and Eric Halton as they describe the effects when others are empowered.

Enabling knowledge transfer through reference to up-to-date exemplars

Les Walton's account, based in the English context, demonstrates how the role of the adviser has changed over time. Relying on examples from the past is unlikely to be sufficient for the future. Indeed, the skilled adviser draws on examples which can create new visions for change or blueprints of practice that will address specific issues for their clients. It's an ever-changing picture and as artificial intelligences emerge, for example, this will present new challenges and opportunities for education advisers.

There is always this contemporary dimension to skilled advising. Note how both Frazer Bailie and Alix Jackson focus on transformational change: each demonstrates complex responsive processes which illustrate renewal in the communities and contexts in which they work. Their 'fit for purpose solutions' illustrate how new solutions can be developed and implemented.

Demonstrating authority and professional credibility with clients

Without authority and professional credibility, the adviser's impact is impaired: this is what we might call 'earned authority'. Dr Louis DeLoreto and Dame Kathy August both show their understanding that contexts are nuanced. They illustrate skills such as determination and persuasion, based on their deep knowledge and experience, as they illustrate that change is a demanding process.

Professional credibility depends upon the way in which the adviser has secured their position through winning hearts and minds through their personal approach and also by demonstrating that they have the skills and knowledge to impact on the situation: this is how they become authoritative in their advisory work.

The following table summarises the learning that this book brings together.

Criterion	Key learning	Chapters
1. Demonstrating personal attributes and skills	The adviser's role can be demanding: there is a need for resilience and determination, often in the face of tension and challenging circumstances. The adviser must apply a range of knowledge and skills to address situations, demonstrating flexibility.	3 4 6 7 8 10 11 12 15 16 17
2. Ability to challenge and work within agreed protocols	The adviser must understand the nature of the commission, their role in the process and the expected outcome. The adviser needs to provide challenge with care when handling complex or highly sensitive situations.	2 3 4 5 6 7 11 14 16 17
3. Acting as an enabler by providing support to drive delivery	The skilled adviser recognises resistance where it is present and uses a range of strategies to overcome it. Empowering colleagues and enabling changes that drive the improvements are essential elements in any advisory support or intervention.	2 3 4 5 6 7 8 9 11 12 13 14 15 16 17

→

Criterion	Key learning	Chapters
4. Enabling knowledge transfer through reference to up-to-date exemplars	Advisers recognise the opportunities in contexts and creatively address issues to bring about change, including where transformational change is possible. Advisers understand both context and evidence to inform development, as well as the active ingredients present in any proposed activity.	8 9 10 13 14 15
5. Demonstrating authority and professional credibility with clients	Effective advisers enable others to be successful by giving them agency. Proving themselves through successful implementation and building long-term lasting professional relationships.	2 3 4 5 6 7 8 10 11 12 13 15 17

It is easy to underestimate both the potential power and influence of advisers as they bring about change in the varying layers of the education system. A judicious approach to their deployment can enhance any organisation. When they surface core issues, identify causal factors, build capacity, work in concert, overcome resistance and lead development they are key agents for change that bring about benefits for children and young people.

> *The vision of the AoEA is that every school, college, and education provider has access to high quality support, advice and challenge, which is independent and focused on improving outcomes for children, schools, and their communities.*
>
> (AoEA)

Reference

Hargreaves, D (2012) *A Self-improving School System: Towards Maturity.* Cambridge: Wolfson College.

Index

Page numbers in *italics* and **bold** refer to figures and tables, respectively.